GRAPHIC SCIENCE BIOGRAPHIES

ISAAC NEWTON AND THE LAWS OF MOTION

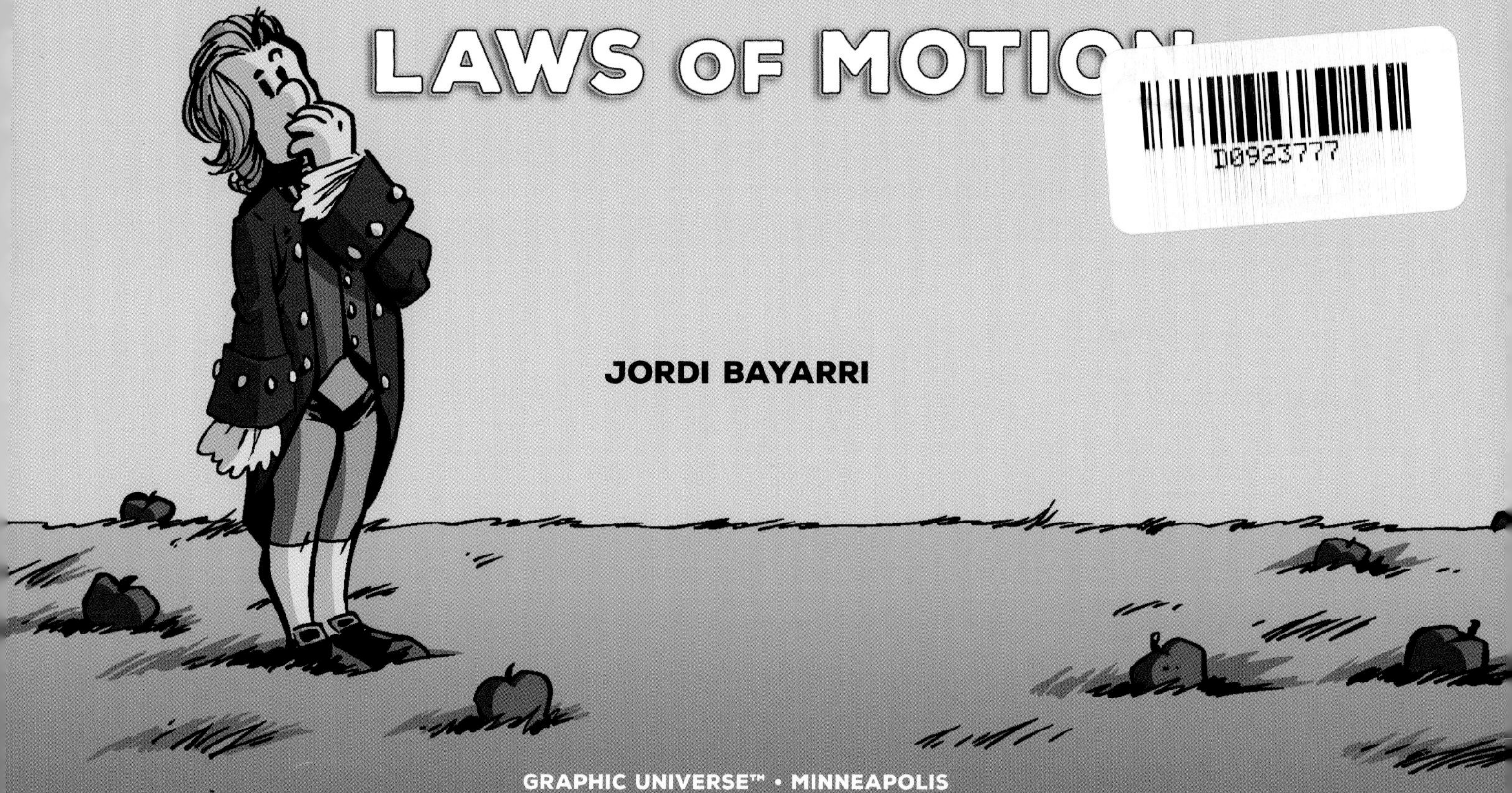

JORDI BAYARRI

GRAPHIC UNIVERSE™ • MINNEAPOLIS

Story and art by Jordi Bayarri
Coloring by Dani Seijas
Historical and scientific consultation by Dr. Tayra M. C. Lanuza-Navarro, PhD in History of Science
Translation by Patricia Ibars and John Wright

First American edition published in 2020 by Graphic Universe™

Graphic Universe™
An imprint of Lerner Publishing Group, Inc.
241 First Avenue North
Minneapolis, MN 55401 USA

For reading levels and more information, look up this title at www.lernerbooks.com.

Image credit: Imagno/Hulton Fine Art Collection/Getty Images, p. 37.

Main body text set in CCDaveGibbonsLower.
Typeface provided by OpenType.

Library of Congress Cataloging-in-Publication Data

Names: Bayarri, Jordi, 1972–author, illustrator.
Title: Isaac Newton and the laws of motion / Jordi Bayarri.
Description: Minneapolis, MN : Graphic Universe, [2020] I Series: Graphic science biographies I Includes bibliographical references and index. I Audience: 10–14. I Audience: 7 to 8.
Identifiers: LCCN 2019009095 I ISBN 9781541578241 (lb ; alk. paper) I ISBN 9781541586987 (pb ; alk. paper) I ISBN 9781541582392 (eb pdf)
Subjects: LCSH: Newton, Isaac, 1642–1727–Comic books, strips, etc. I Newton, Isaac, 1642–1727 –Juvenile literature. I Physicists–Great Britain–Biography–Comic books, strips, etc. I Physicists –Great Britain–Biography–Juvenile literature. I Gravity–Comic books, strips, etc. I Gravity–Juvenile literature.
Classification: LCC QC16.N7 B39 2020 I DDC 530.092 [B] –dc23

LC record available at https://lccn.loc.gov/2019009095

Manufactured in the United States of America
1-46931-47809-5/16/2019

CONTENTS

ISAAC NEWTON WAS BORN ON DECEMBER 25, 1642, IN WOOLSTHORPE-BY-COLSTERWORTH, ENGLAND.

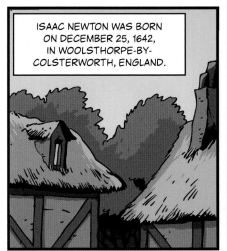

AT THE AGE OF TWELVE, HE ATTENDED SCHOOL IN NEARBY GRANTHAM. HE LIVED WITH THE LOCAL APOTHECARY, WHO TAUGHT HIM CHEMISTRY.

HE ALSO HAD HIS OWN TOOLS. HE USED THEM TO BUILD TOYS.

OH, HOW PRETTY! IS THIS FOR ME?

DID YOU HEAR ABOUT THE MILL THEY'RE BUILDING?

COME ON, LET'S TAKE A LOOK!

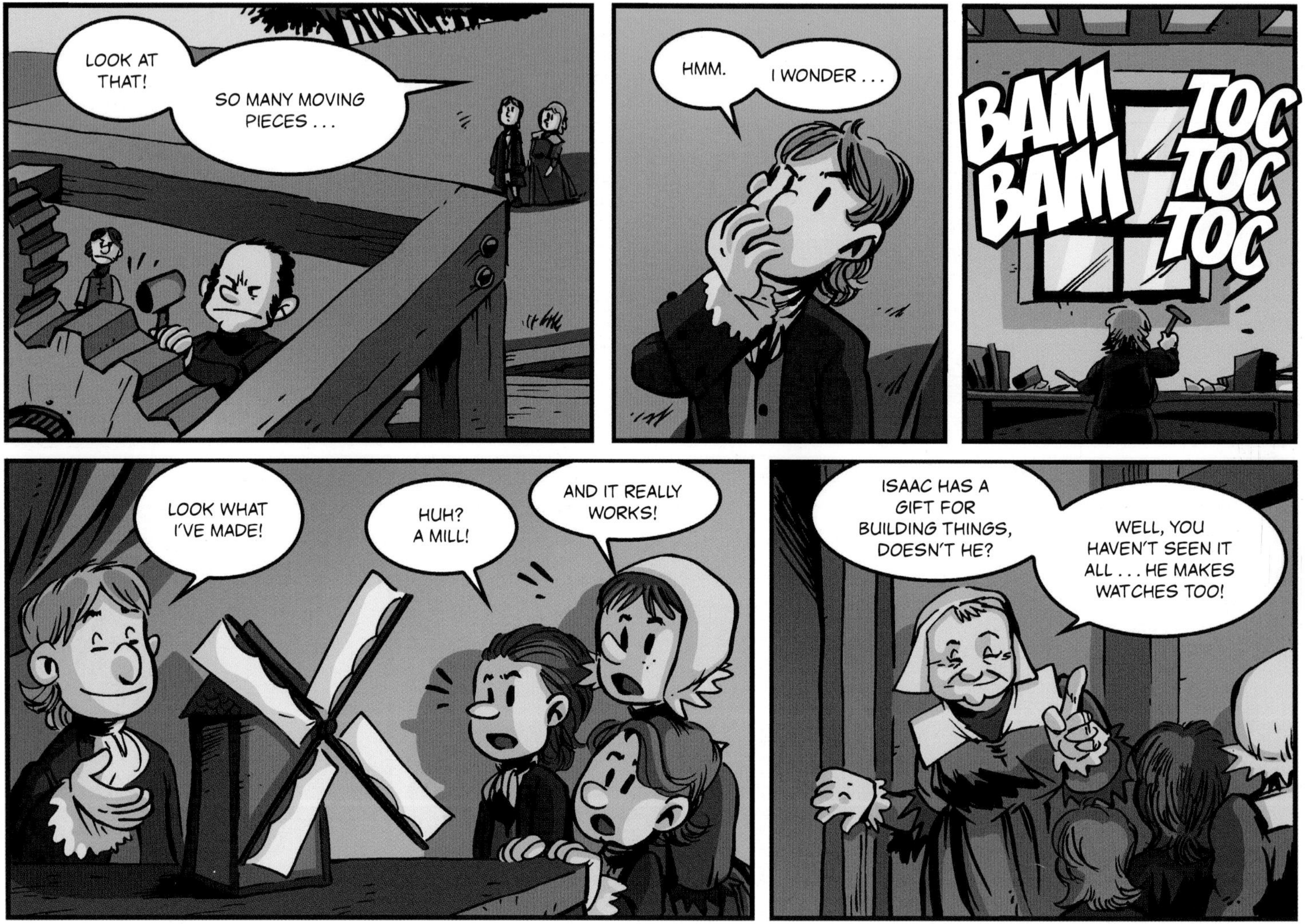
LOOK AT THAT!
SO MANY MOVING PIECES . . .
HMM.
I WONDER . . .
BAM BAM
TOC TOC TOC
LOOK WHAT I'VE MADE!
HUH? A MILL!
AND IT REALLY WORKS!
ISAAC HAS A GIFT FOR BUILDING THINGS, DOESN'T HE?
WELL, YOU HAVEN'T SEEN IT ALL . . . HE MAKES WATCHES TOO!

TAKE A LOOK AT THIS WATER CLOCK.

IT WORKS SO WELL OUR WHOLE FAMILY USES IT.

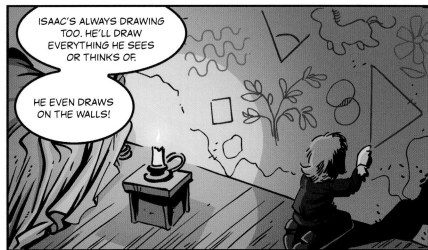

ISAAC'S ALWAYS DRAWING TOO. HE'LL DRAW EVERYTHING HE SEES OR THINKS OF.

HE EVEN DRAWS ON THE WALLS!

HANNAH, YOUR SON ISAAC IS VERY CLEVER. HE SHOULD REALLY GO TO UNIVERSITY.

I AGREE, MY DEAR SISTER.

"YOU'RE RIGHT. PERHAPS . . . CAMBRIDGE?"

1661

WELCOME TO TRINITY COLLEGE, MR. NEWTON.

THE RULES OF THE UNIVERSITY OF CAMBRIDGE STATE THAT AFTER OBTAINING YOUR MASTER'S DEGREE AND BECOMING A FELLOW, YOU MUST BE ORDAINED AS A PRIEST WITHIN SEVEN YEARS.

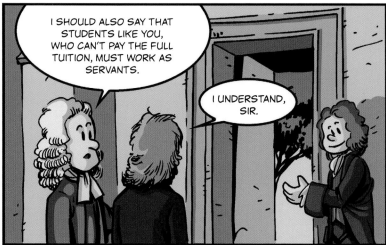

I SHOULD ALSO SAY THAT STUDENTS LIKE YOU, WHO CAN'T PAY THE FULL TUITION, MUST WORK AS SERVANTS.

I UNDERSTAND, SIR.

AH! HERE'S YOUR RESIDENCE. YOU'LL LIVE HERE WHILE YOU'RE AT CAMBRIDGE.

NOW ALLOW ME TO INTRODUCE YOU TO YOUR ROOMMATE.

JOHN WICKINS. PLEASED TO MEET YOU.

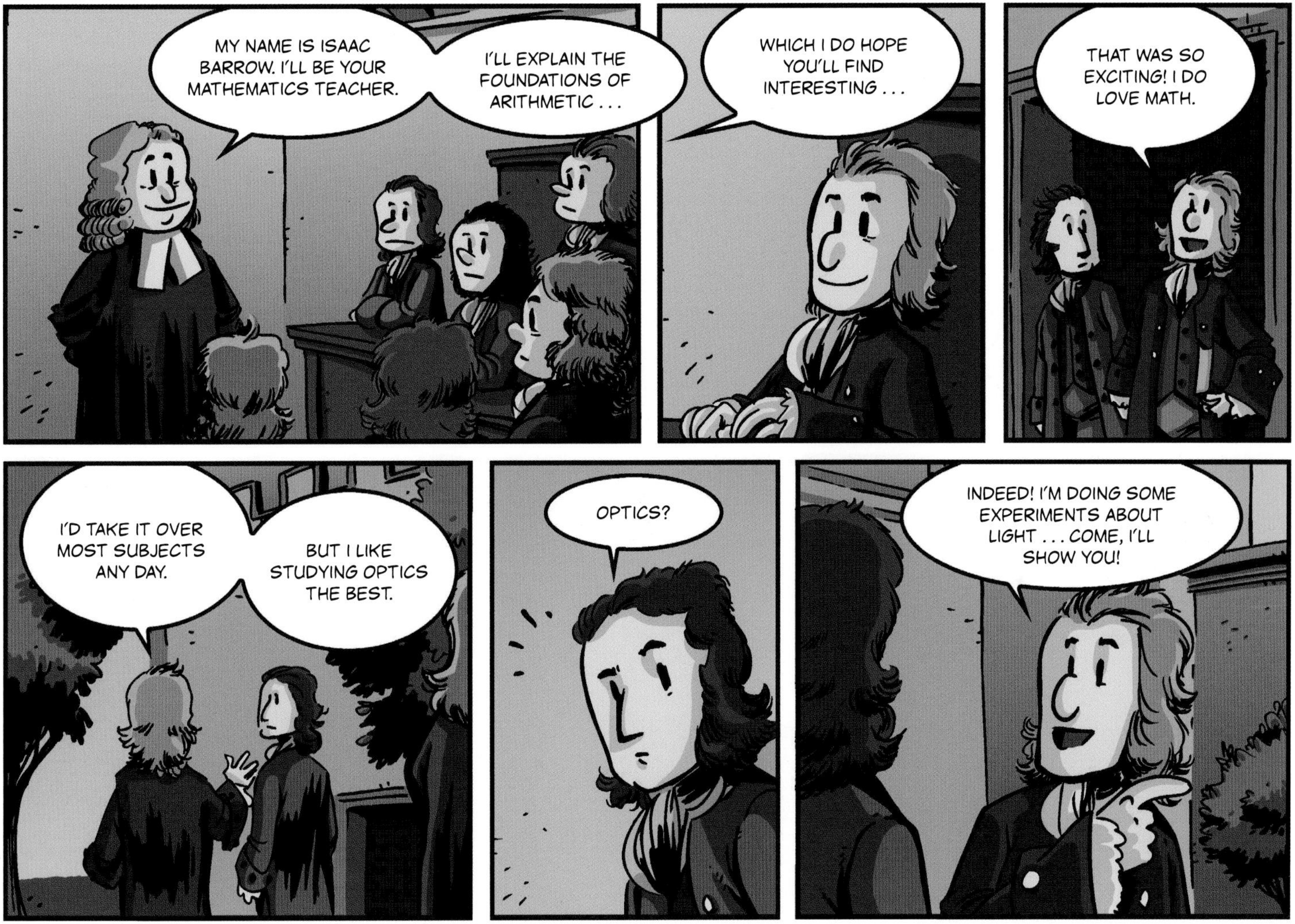
MY NAME IS ISAAC BARROW. I'LL BE YOUR MATHEMATICS TEACHER.
I'LL EXPLAIN THE FOUNDATIONS OF ARITHMETIC . . .
WHICH I DO HOPE YOU'LL FIND INTERESTING . . .
THAT WAS SO EXCITING! I DO LOVE MATH.
I'D TAKE IT OVER MOST SUBJECTS ANY DAY.
BUT I LIKE STUDYING OPTICS THE BEST.
OPTICS?
INDEED! I'M DOING SOME EXPERIMENTS ABOUT LIGHT . . . COME, I'LL SHOW YOU!

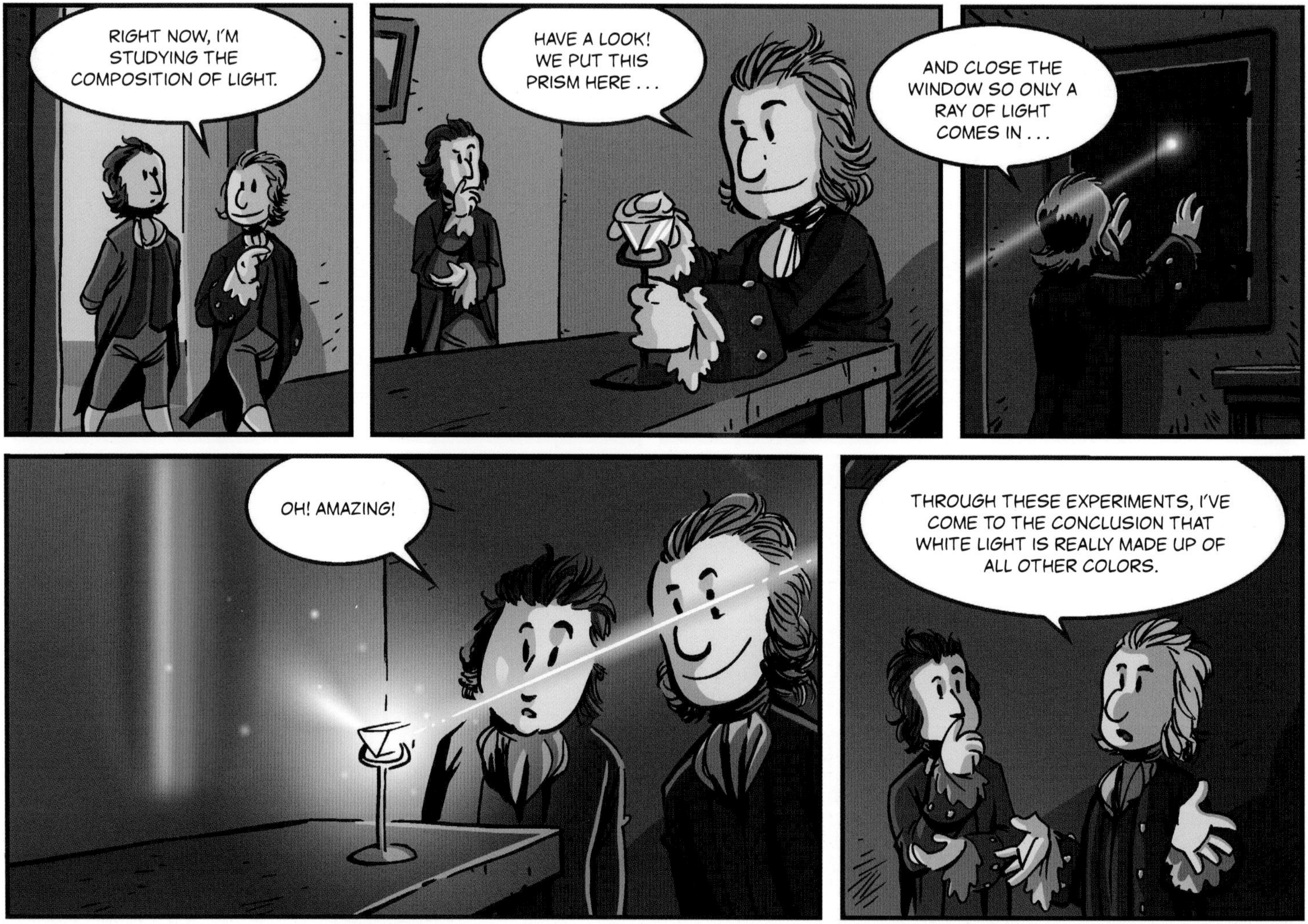
RIGHT NOW, I'M STUDYING THE COMPOSITION OF LIGHT.
HAVE A LOOK! WE PUT THIS PRISM HERE . . .
AND CLOSE THE WINDOW SO ONLY A RAY OF LIGHT COMES IN . . .
OH! AMAZING!
THROUGH THESE EXPERIMENTS, I'VE COME TO THE CONCLUSION THAT WHITE LIGHT IS REALLY MADE UP OF ALL OTHER COLORS.

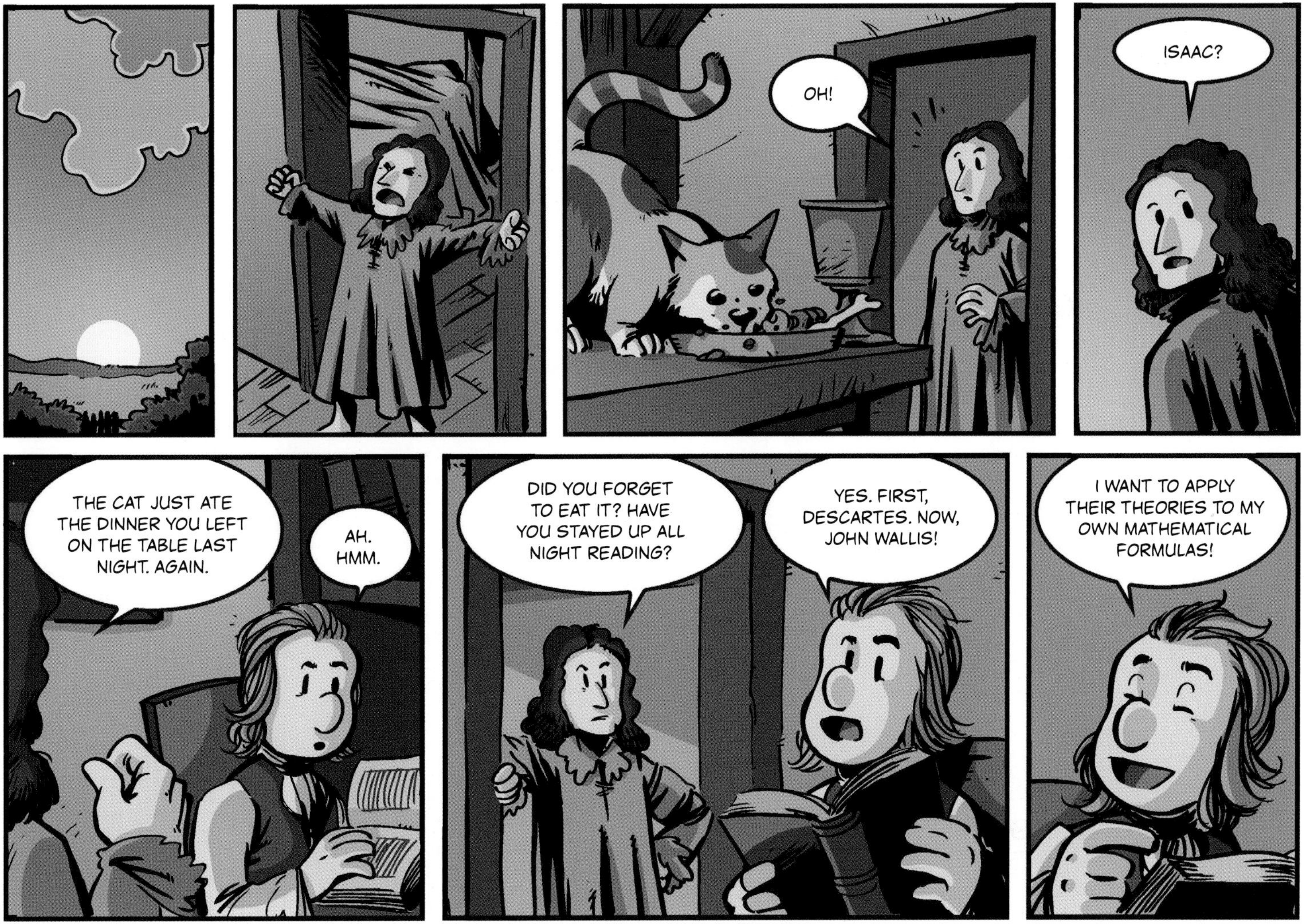
OH!
ISAAC?
THE CAT JUST ATE THE DINNER YOU LEFT ON THE TABLE LAST NIGHT. AGAIN.
AH. HMM.
DID YOU FORGET TO EAT IT? HAVE YOU STAYED UP ALL NIGHT READING?
YES. FIRST, DESCARTES. NOW, JOHN WALLIS!
I WANT TO APPLY THEIR THEORIES TO MY OWN MATHEMATICAL FORMULAS!

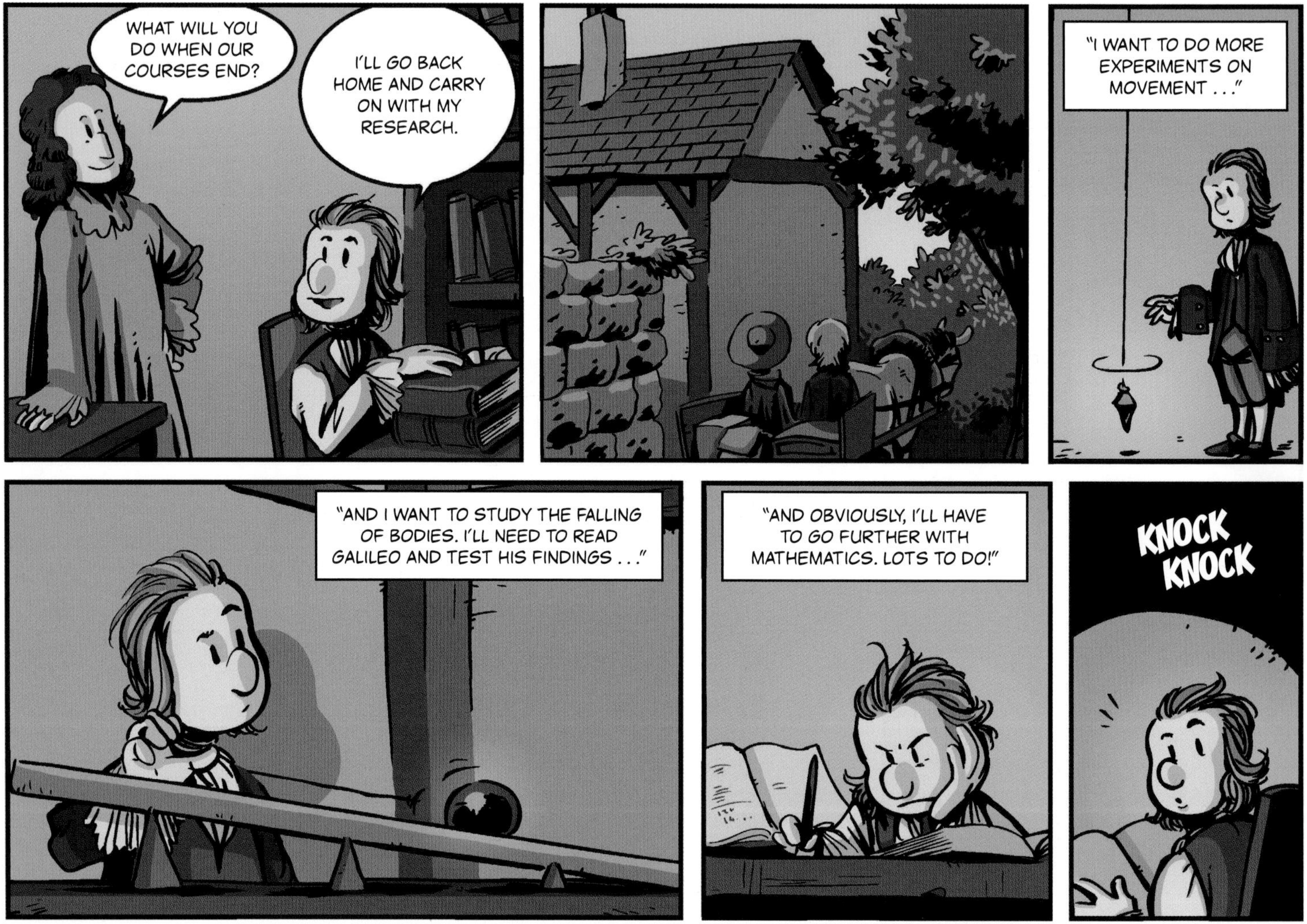
WHAT WILL YOU DO WHEN OUR COURSES END?
I'LL GO BACK HOME AND CARRY ON WITH MY RESEARCH.
"I WANT TO DO MORE EXPERIMENTS ON MOVEMENT . . ."
"AND I WANT TO STUDY THE FALLING OF BODIES. I'LL NEED TO READ GALILEO AND TEST HIS FINDINGS . . ."
"AND OBVIOUSLY, I'LL HAVE TO GO FURTHER WITH MATHEMATICS. LOTS TO DO!"
KNOCK KNOCK

MR. NEWTON! YOU HAVE AN URGENT LETTER FROM CAMBRIDGE.

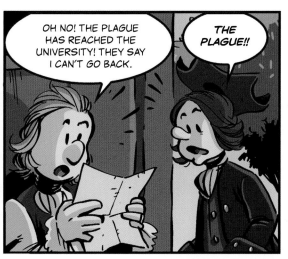

OH NO! THE PLAGUE HAS REACHED THE UNIVERSITY! THEY SAY I CAN'T GO BACK.

THE PLAGUE!!

WELL, NO MATTER. THIS WAY, I CAN STAY HERE AND CARRY ON WITH MY WORK . . .

I'M VERY CLOSE TO DEVELOPING A METHOD TO CALCULATE QUADRATURES AND TANGENTS.

I . . . DON'T UNDERSTAND . . .

"I'LL CALL IT THE METHOD OF FLUXIONS."

YAWWWN. TIME FOR A STROLL AROUND THE APPLE TREES.

ACCORDING TO MY EXPERIMENTS ON THE MOVEMENT OF OBJECTS, EVERYTHING DEPENDS ON FORCE.

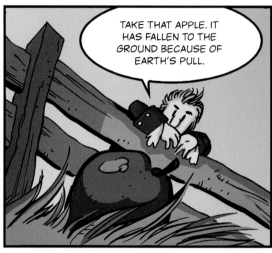

TAKE THAT APPLE. IT HAS FALLEN TO THE GROUND BECAUSE OF EARTH'S PULL.

BUT WHY DOESN'T THE MOON ATTRACT IT TOO? BECAUSE IT'S TOO FAR AWAY? BECAUSE THE MOON'S SMALLER?

DOES EARTH ATTRACT THE MOON? DO THEY BOTH ATTRACT EACH OTHER? WHAT ABOUT THE SUN?

I'LL HAVE TO KEEP THINKING . . .

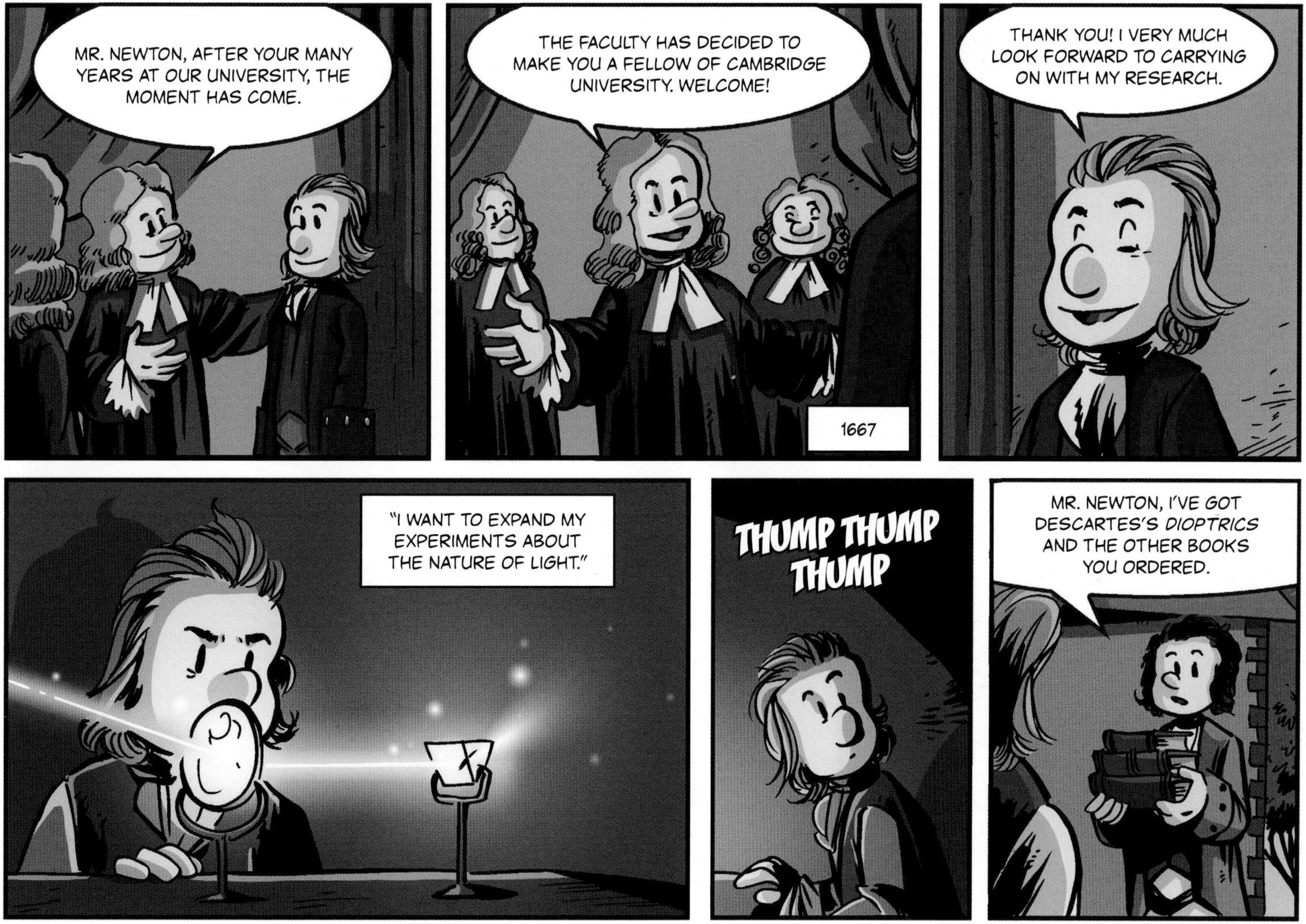
MR. NEWTON, AFTER YOUR MANY YEARS AT OUR UNIVERSITY, THE MOMENT HAS COME.
THE FACULTY HAS DECIDED TO MAKE YOU A FELLOW OF CAMBRIDGE UNIVERSITY. WELCOME!
1667
THANK YOU! I VERY MUCH LOOK FORWARD TO CARRYING ON WITH MY RESEARCH.
"I WANT TO EXPAND MY EXPERIMENTS ABOUT THE NATURE OF LIGHT."
THUMP THUMP THUMP
MR. NEWTON, I'VE GOT DESCARTES'S *DIOPTRICS* AND THE OTHER BOOKS YOU ORDERED.

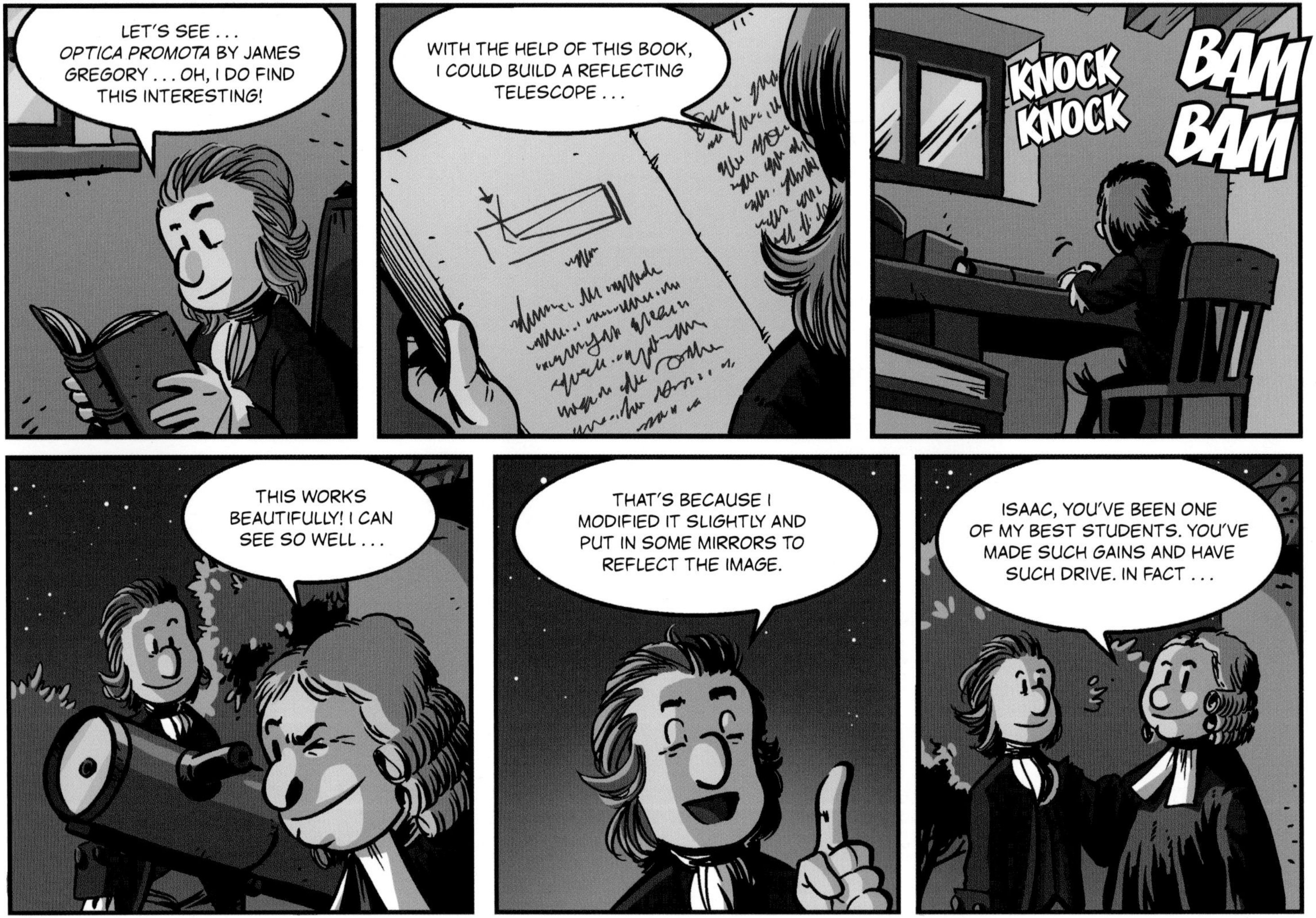

LET'S SEE . . . *OPTICA PROMOTA* BY JAMES GREGORY . . . OH, I DO FIND THIS INTERESTING!
WITH THE HELP OF THIS BOOK, I COULD BUILD A REFLECTING TELESCOPE . . .
KNOCK KNOCK
BAM BAM
THIS WORKS BEAUTIFULLY! I CAN SEE SO WELL . . .
THAT'S BECAUSE I MODIFIED IT SLIGHTLY AND PUT IN SOME MIRRORS TO REFLECT THE IMAGE.
ISAAC, YOU'VE BEEN ONE OF MY BEST STUDENTS. YOU'VE MADE SUCH GAINS AND HAVE SUCH DRIVE. IN FACT . . .

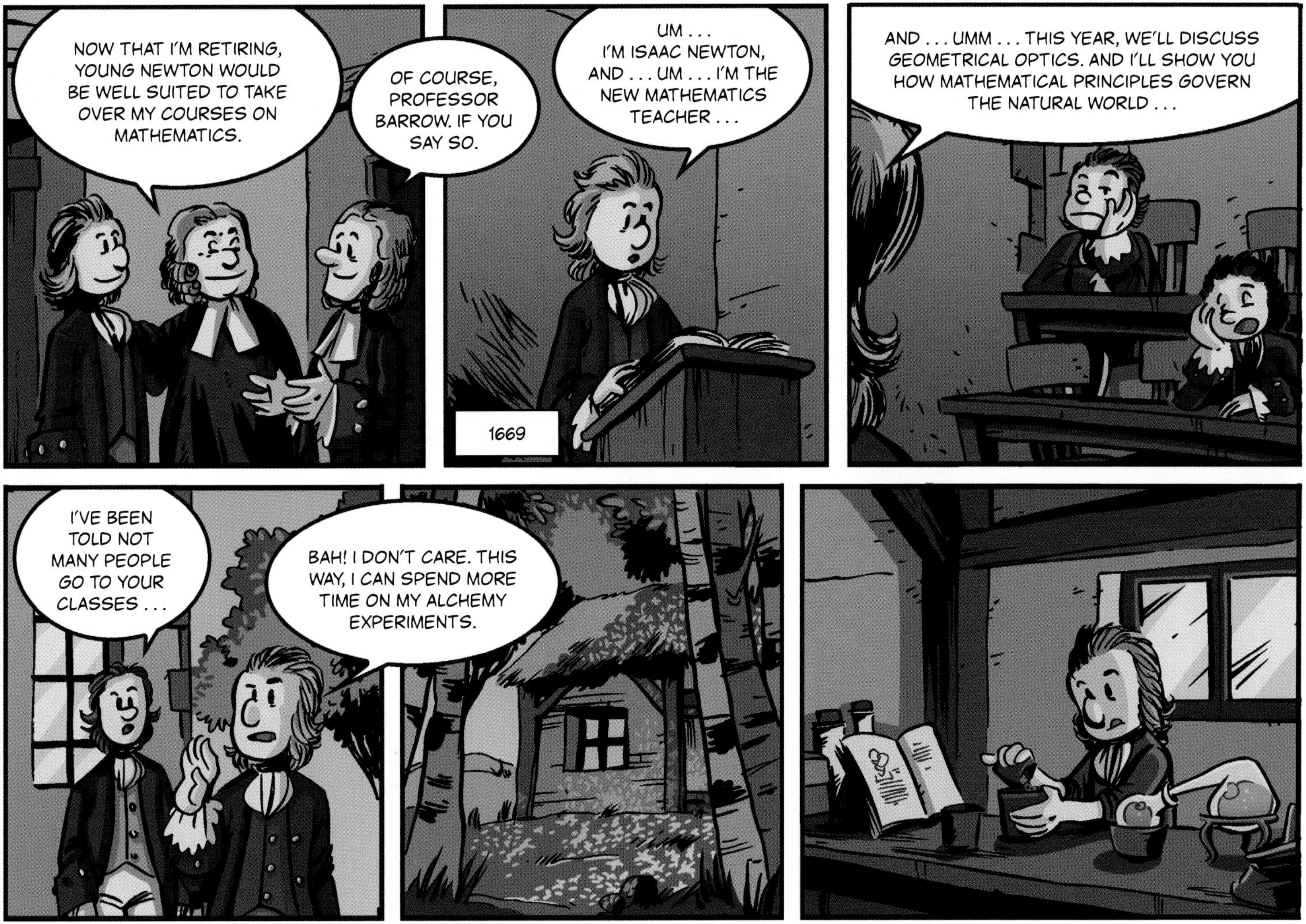
NOW THAT I'M RETIRING, YOUNG NEWTON WOULD BE WELL SUITED TO TAKE OVER MY COURSES ON MATHEMATICS.
OF COURSE, PROFESSOR BARROW. IF YOU SAY SO.
UM . . . I'M ISAAC NEWTON, AND . . . UM . . . I'M THE NEW MATHEMATICS TEACHER . . .
1669
AND . . . UMM . . . THIS YEAR, WE'LL DISCUSS GEOMETRICAL OPTICS. AND I'LL SHOW YOU HOW MATHEMATICAL PRINCIPLES GOVERN THE NATURAL WORLD . . .
I'VE BEEN TOLD NOT MANY PEOPLE GO TO YOUR CLASSES . . .
BAH! I DON'T CARE. THIS WAY, I CAN SPEND MORE TIME ON MY ALCHEMY EXPERIMENTS.

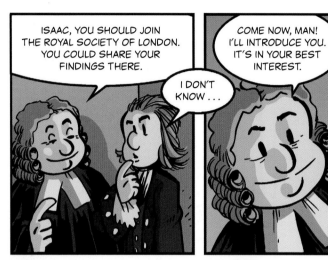

ISAAC, YOU SHOULD JOIN THE ROYAL SOCIETY OF LONDON. YOU COULD SHARE YOUR FINDINGS THERE.

I DON'T KNOW . . .

COME NOW, MAN! I'LL INTRODUCE YOU. IT'S IN YOUR BEST INTEREST.

GENTLEMEN, I PRESENT TO YOU ISAAC NEWTON. HE'S A PROFESSOR AT TRINITY COLLEGE WITH A TIRELESS MIND. AN EXCELLENT CANDIDATE FOR OUR SOCIETY!

MR. NEWTON IS INTERESTED IN MATHEMATICS, FALLING BODIES, AND OPTICS.

HE HAS CONSTRUCTED THIS REFLECTING TELESCOPE, AMONG OTHER THINGS.

HMM. INTERESTING.

WELCOME TO THE ROYAL SOCIETY, MR. NEWTON!

THANK YOU!

1672

GENTLEMEN, DURING THIS SESSION, WE'LL DEBATE THE ARTICLE MR. NEWTON SENT US ON THE COMPOSITION OF LIGHT.

HE'S MADE SOME VERY INTERESTING CONCLUSIONS.

IT MUST BE PUBLISHED IN OUR JOURNAL SO EVERYONE CAN READ IT.

OH! THIS IS OUTRAGEOUS!

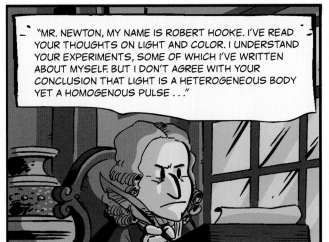

"MR. NEWTON, MY NAME IS ROBERT HOOKE. I'VE READ YOUR THOUGHTS ON LIGHT AND COLOR. I UNDERSTAND YOUR EXPERIMENTS, SOME OF WHICH I'VE WRITTEN ABOUT MYSELF. BUT I DON'T AGREE WITH YOUR CONCLUSION THAT LIGHT IS A HETEROGENEOUS BODY YET A HOMOGENOUS PULSE . . ."

WELL!

"MR. HOOKE, WITHOUT GOING TOO FAR INTO THE NATURE OF LIGHT, I MUST SAY THAT EXPERIMENTS WITH A SECOND PRISM SHOW THAT LIGHT CONSISTS OF RAYS OF DIFFERENT REFRACTION AND THAT WHITE IS A MIXTURE OF COLORS."

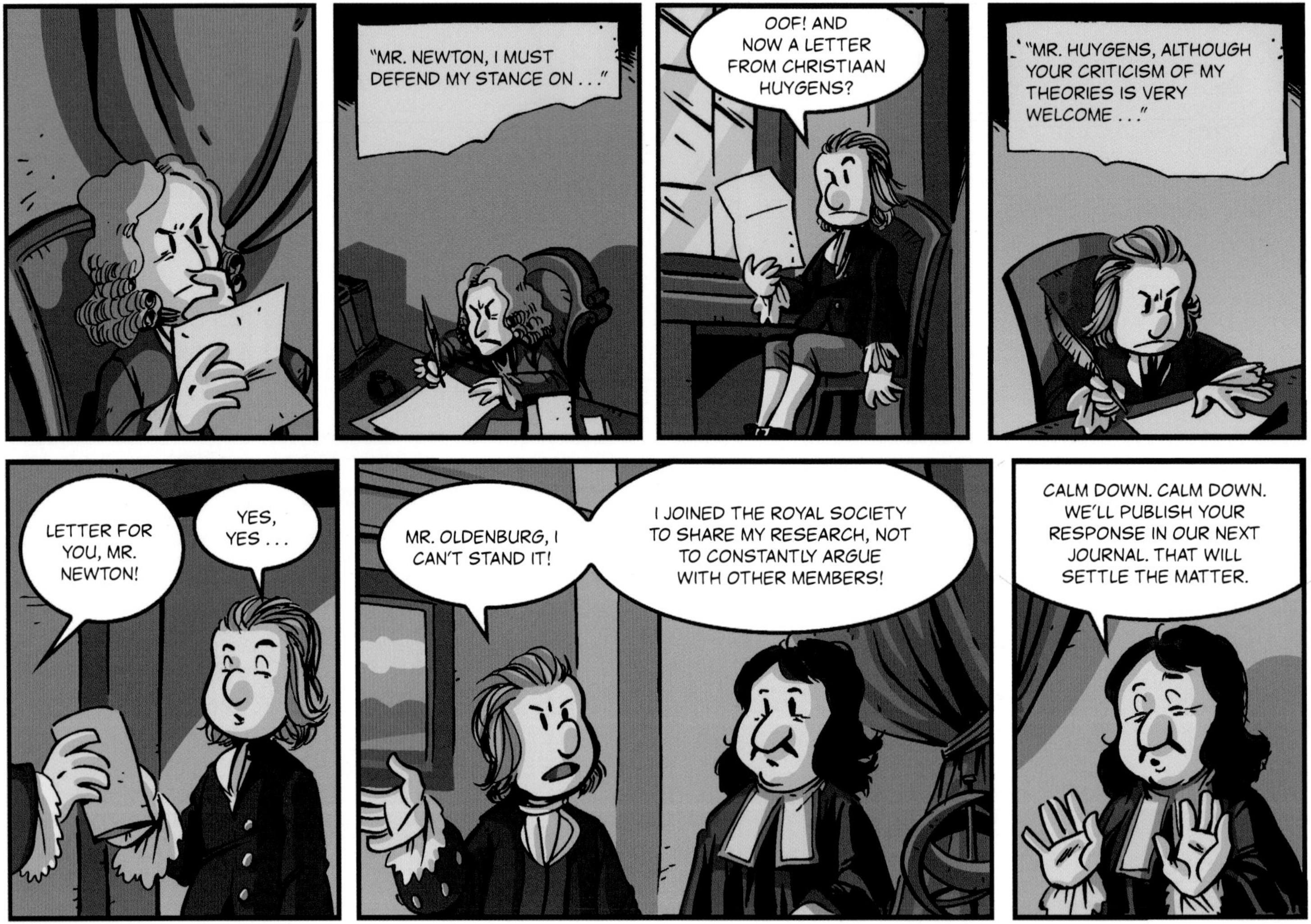
"MR. NEWTON, I MUST DEFEND MY STANCE ON . . ."
OOF! AND NOW A LETTER FROM CHRISTIAAN HUYGENS?
"MR. HUYGENS, ALTHOUGH YOUR CRITICISM OF MY THEORIES IS VERY WELCOME . . ."
LETTER FOR YOU, MR. NEWTON!
YES, YES . . .
MR. OLDENBURG, I CAN'T STAND IT!
I JOINED THE ROYAL SOCIETY TO SHARE MY RESEARCH, NOT TO CONSTANTLY ARGUE WITH OTHER MEMBERS!
CALM DOWN. CALM DOWN. WE'LL PUBLISH YOUR RESPONSE IN OUR NEXT JOURNAL. THAT WILL SETTLE THE MATTER.

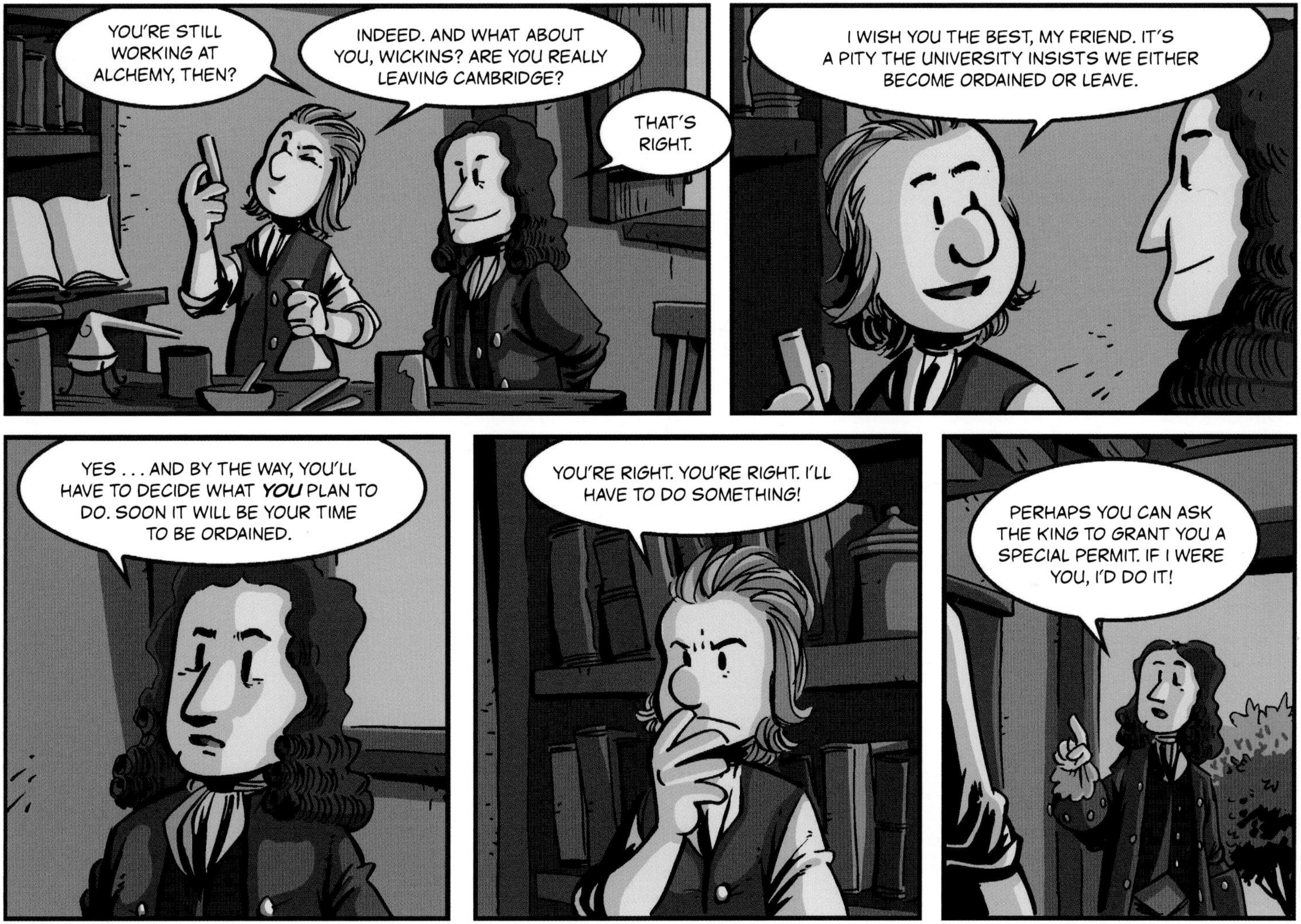
YOU'RE STILL WORKING AT ALCHEMY, THEN?
INDEED. AND WHAT ABOUT YOU, WICKINS? ARE YOU REALLY LEAVING CAMBRIDGE?
THAT'S RIGHT.
I WISH YOU THE BEST, MY FRIEND. IT'S A PITY THE UNIVERSITY INSISTS WE EITHER BECOME ORDAINED OR LEAVE.
YES . . . AND BY THE WAY, YOU'LL HAVE TO DECIDE WHAT ***YOU*** PLAN TO DO. SOON IT WILL BE YOUR TIME TO BE ORDAINED.
YOU'RE RIGHT. YOU'RE RIGHT. I'LL HAVE TO DO SOMETHING!
PERHAPS YOU CAN ASK THE KING TO GRANT YOU A SPECIAL PERMIT. IF I WERE YOU, I'D DO IT!

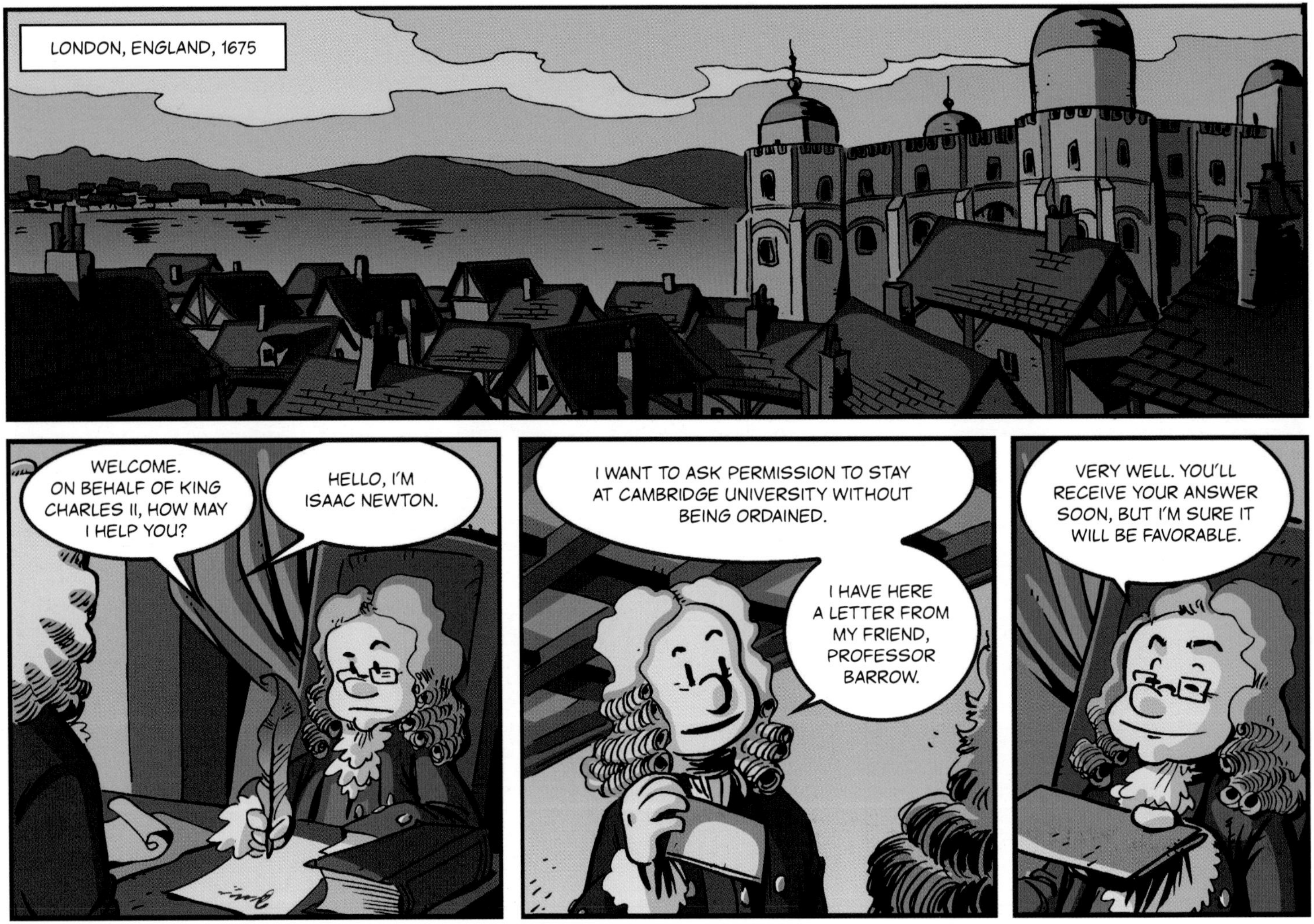
LONDON, ENGLAND, 1675
WELCOME. ON BEHALF OF KING CHARLES II, HOW MAY I HELP YOU?
HELLO, I'M ISAAC NEWTON.
I WANT TO ASK PERMISSION TO STAY AT CAMBRIDGE UNIVERSITY WITHOUT BEING ORDAINED.
I HAVE HERE A LETTER FROM MY FRIEND, PROFESSOR BARROW.
VERY WELL. YOU'LL RECEIVE YOUR ANSWER SOON, BUT I'M SURE IT WILL BE FAVORABLE.

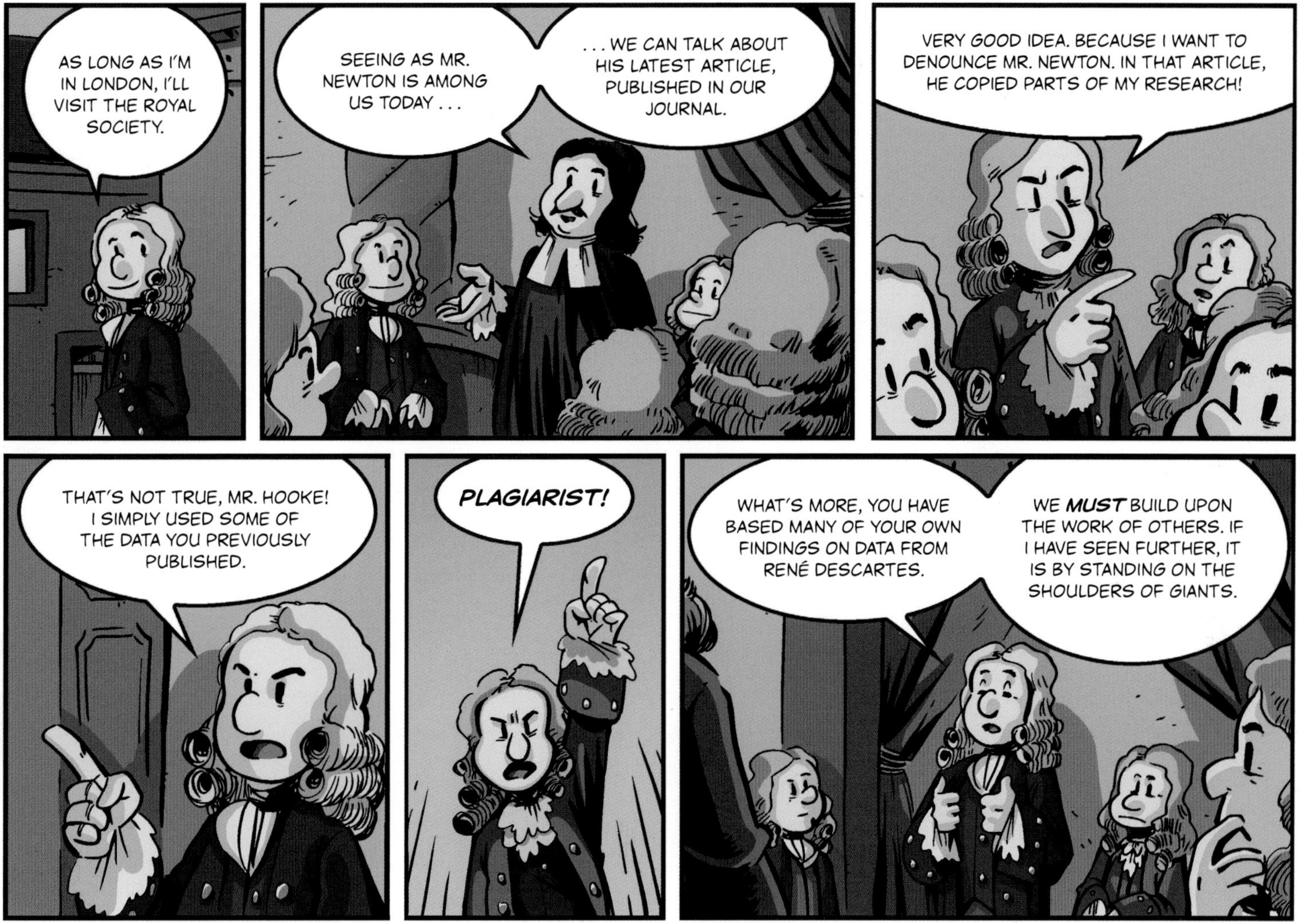
AS LONG AS I'M IN LONDON, I'LL VISIT THE ROYAL SOCIETY.
SEEING AS MR. NEWTON IS AMONG US TODAY . . .
. . . WE CAN TALK ABOUT HIS LATEST ARTICLE, PUBLISHED IN OUR JOURNAL.
VERY GOOD IDEA. BECAUSE I WANT TO DENOUNCE MR. NEWTON. IN THAT ARTICLE, HE COPIED PARTS OF MY RESEARCH!
THAT'S NOT TRUE, MR. HOOKE! I SIMPLY USED SOME OF THE DATA YOU PREVIOUSLY PUBLISHED.
PLAGIARIST!
WHAT'S MORE, YOU HAVE BASED MANY OF YOUR OWN FINDINGS ON DATA FROM RENÉ DESCARTES.
WE MUST BUILD UPON THE WORK OF OTHERS. IF I HAVE SEEN FURTHER, IT IS BY STANDING ON THE SHOULDERS OF GIANTS.

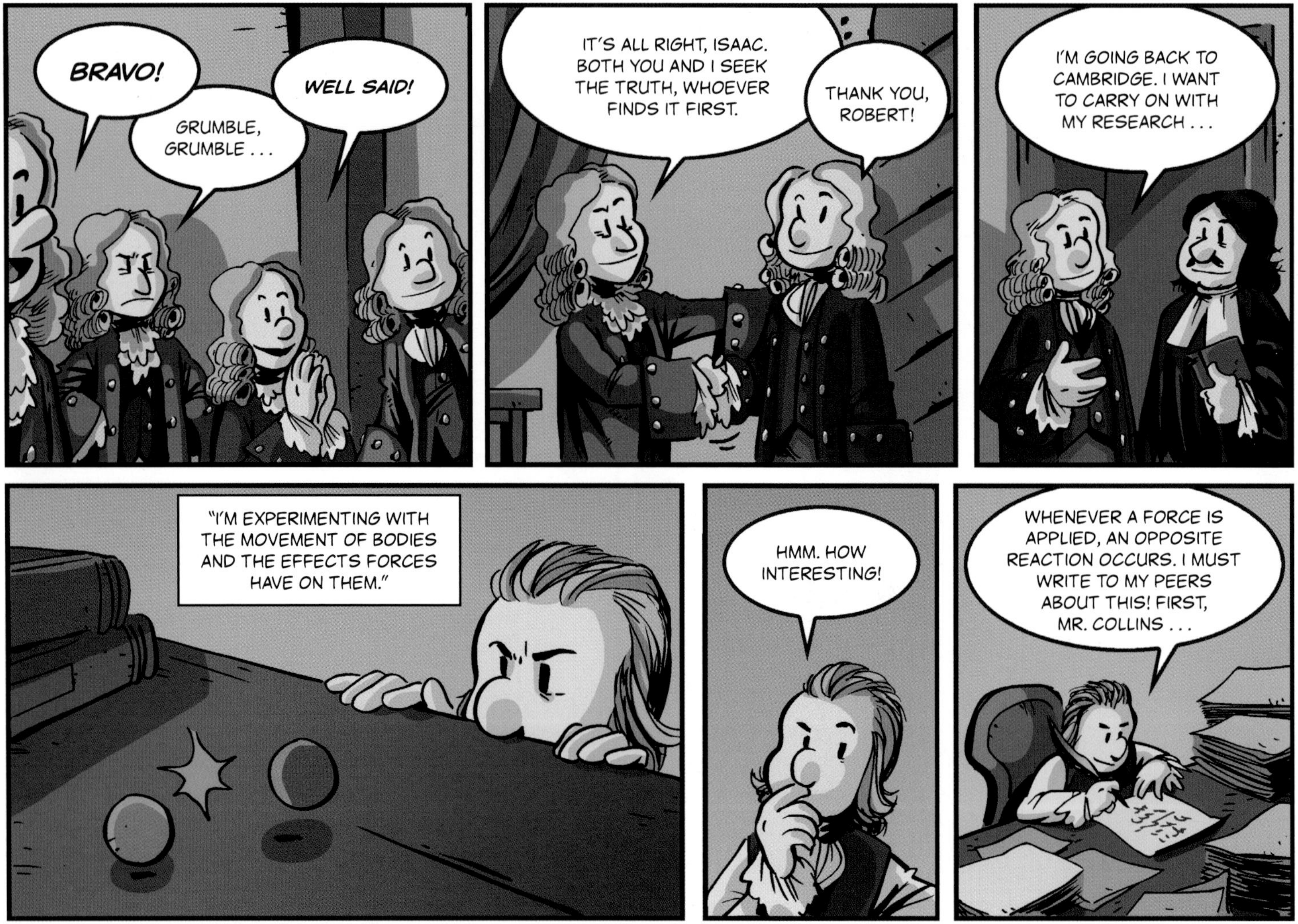
BRAVO!
GRUMBLE, GRUMBLE . . .
WELL SAID!
IT'S ALL RIGHT, ISAAC. BOTH YOU AND I SEEK THE TRUTH, WHOEVER FINDS IT FIRST.
THANK YOU, ROBERT!
I'M GOING BACK TO CAMBRIDGE. I WANT TO CARRY ON WITH MY RESEARCH . . .
"I'M EXPERIMENTING WITH THE MOVEMENT OF BODIES AND THE EFFECTS FORCES HAVE ON THEM."
HMM. HOW INTERESTING!
WHENEVER A FORCE IS APPLIED, AN OPPOSITE REACTION OCCURS. I MUST WRITE TO MY PEERS ABOUT THIS! FIRST, MR. COLLINS . . .

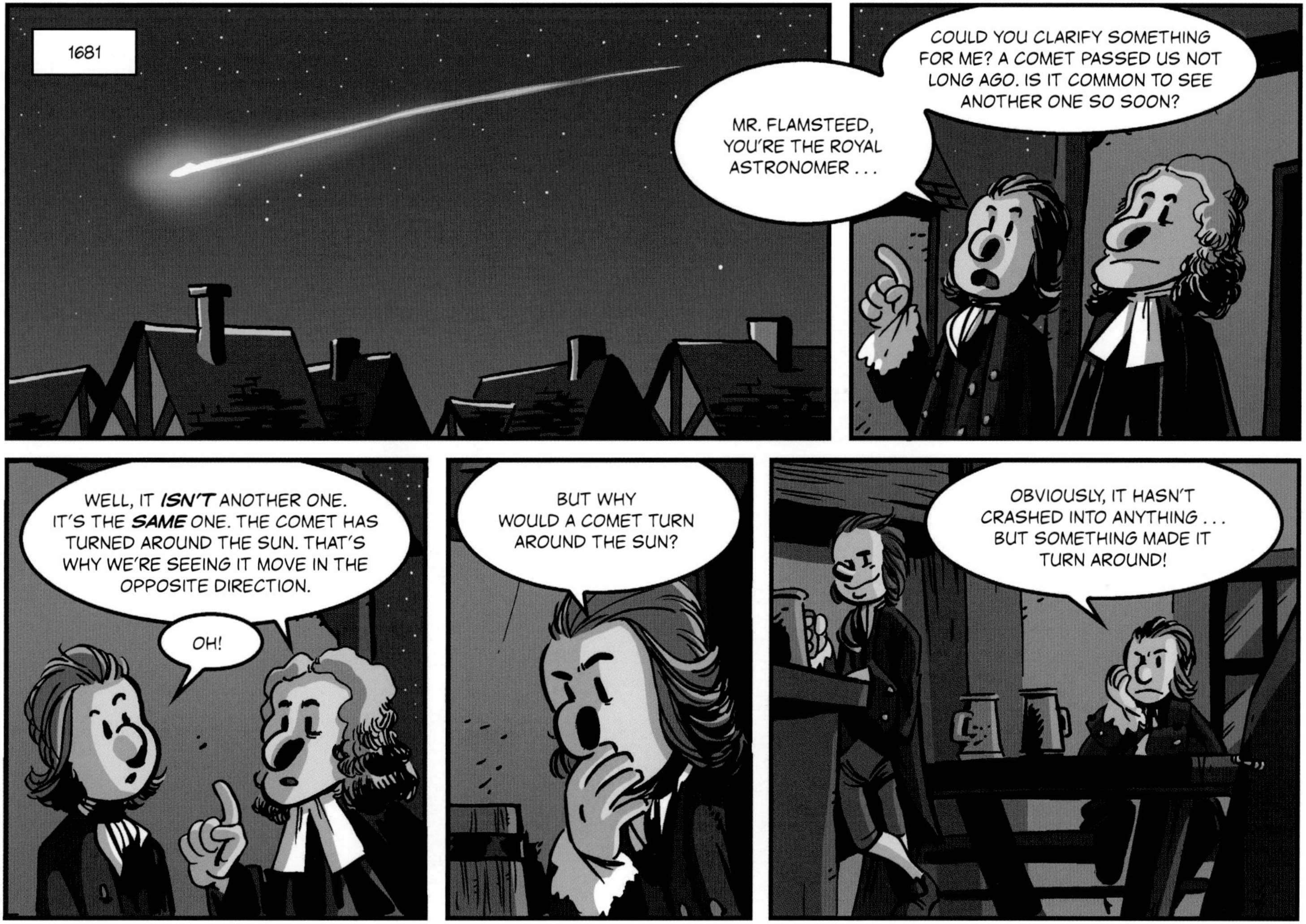
1681
MR. FLAMSTEED, YOU'RE THE ROYAL ASTRONOMER . . .
COULD YOU CLARIFY SOMETHING FOR ME? A COMET PASSED US NOT LONG AGO. IS IT COMMON TO SEE ANOTHER ONE SO SOON?
WELL, IT *ISN'T* ANOTHER ONE. IT'S THE *SAME* ONE. THE COMET HAS TURNED AROUND THE SUN. THAT'S WHY WE'RE SEEING IT MOVE IN THE OPPOSITE DIRECTION.
OH!
BUT WHY WOULD A COMET TURN AROUND THE SUN?
OBVIOUSLY, IT HASN'T CRASHED INTO ANYTHING . . . BUT SOMETHING MADE IT TURN AROUND!

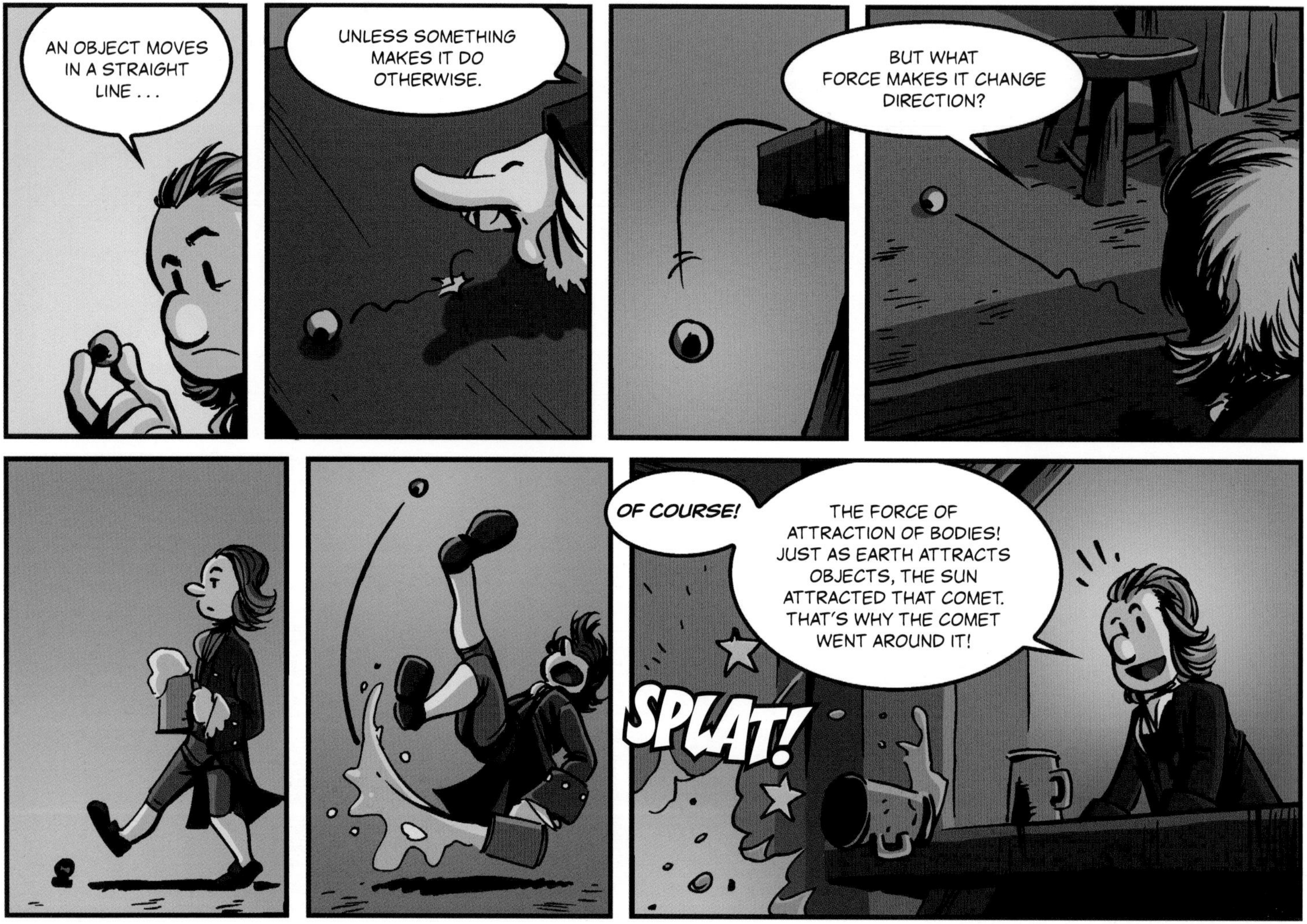
AN OBJECT MOVES IN A STRAIGHT LINE . . .
UNLESS SOMETHING MAKES IT DO OTHERWISE.
BUT WHAT FORCE MAKES IT CHANGE DIRECTION?
OF COURSE!
SPLAT!
THE FORCE OF ATTRACTION OF BODIES! JUST AS EARTH ATTRACTS OBJECTS, THE SUN ATTRACTED THAT COMET. THAT'S WHY THE COMET WENT AROUND IT!

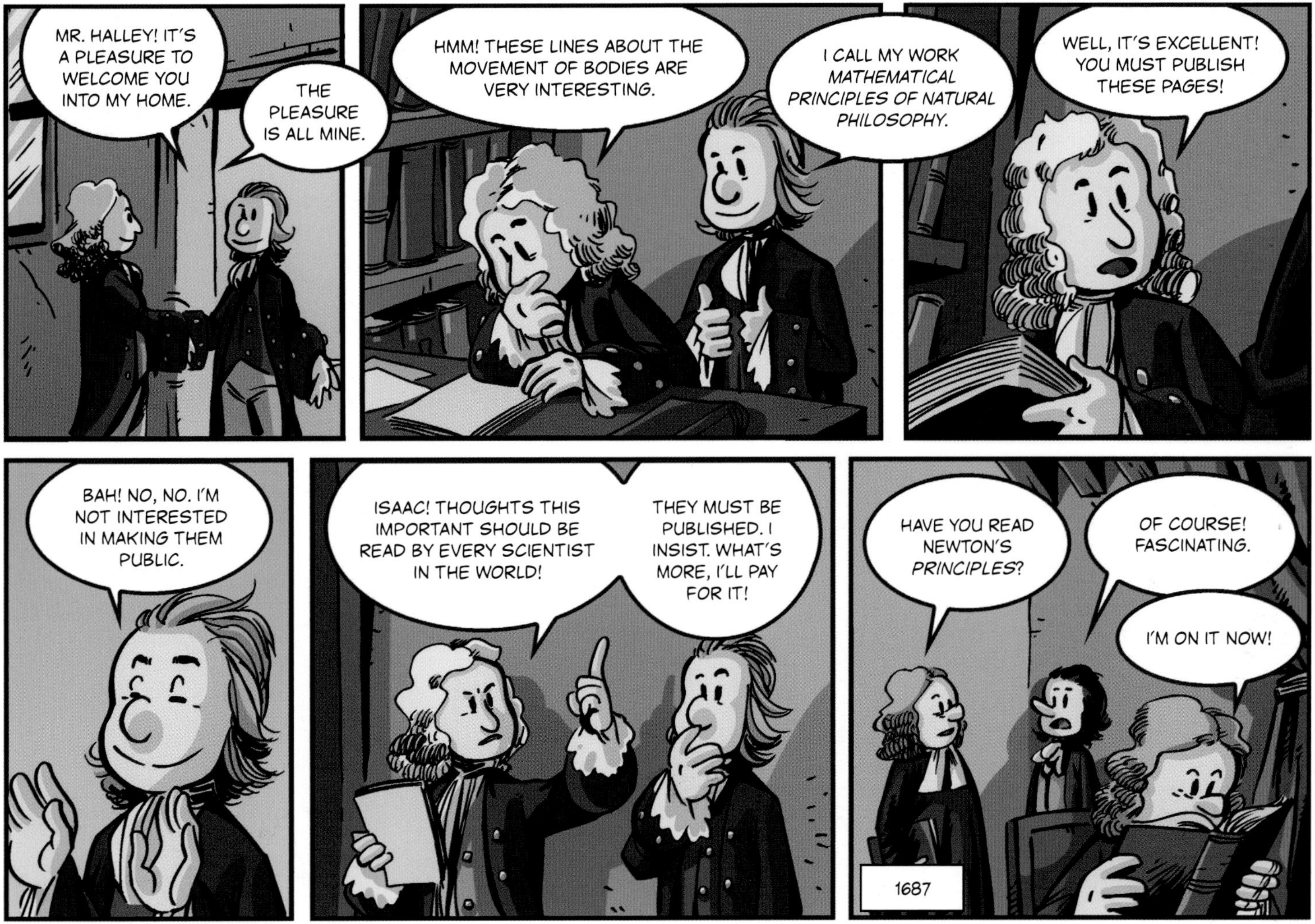
MR. HALLEY! IT'S A PLEASURE TO WELCOME YOU INTO MY HOME.
THE PLEASURE IS ALL MINE.
HMM! THESE LINES ABOUT THE MOVEMENT OF BODIES ARE VERY INTERESTING.
I CALL MY WORK *MATHEMATICAL PRINCIPLES OF NATURAL PHILOSOPHY.*
WELL, IT'S EXCELLENT! YOU MUST PUBLISH THESE PAGES!
BAH! NO, NO. I'M NOT INTERESTED IN MAKING THEM PUBLIC.
ISAAC! THOUGHTS THIS IMPORTANT SHOULD BE READ BY EVERY SCIENTIST IN THE WORLD!
THEY MUST BE PUBLISHED. I INSIST. WHAT'S MORE, I'LL PAY FOR IT!
1687
HAVE YOU READ NEWTON'S *PRINCIPLES?*
OF COURSE! FASCINATING.
I'M ON IT NOW!

WHAT I PROPOSE IN MY WORK IS THE EXISTENCE OF THREE LAWS THAT APPLY TO THE MOTION OF OBJECTS.

ALLOW ME TO EXPLAIN.

FIRST, AN OBJECT STAYS AT REST--OR IN UNIFORM MOTION, IN A STRAIGHT LINE-- UNLESS FORCES IMPRESSED UPON IT MAKE THE OBJECT CHANGE ITS STATE.

SECOND, WHEN A DRIVING FORCE ACTS ON AN OBJECT, IT CHANGES THE OBJECT'S SPEED AND DIRECTION. THIS CHANGE IN MOTION IS PROPORTIONAL TO THE DRIVING FORCE. IT FOLLOWS THE STRAIGHT LINE FROM WHICH THE FORCE IS IMPRESSED.

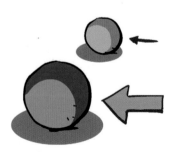

THIRD, FOR EVERY ACTION, THERE IS AN EQUAL AND OPPOSITE REACTION.

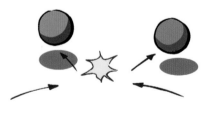

WHAT'S MORE, I'M CONVINCED THESE THREE LAWS--TOGETHER WITH THAT OF GRAVITY--RULE THE MOTION OF THE UNIVERSE.

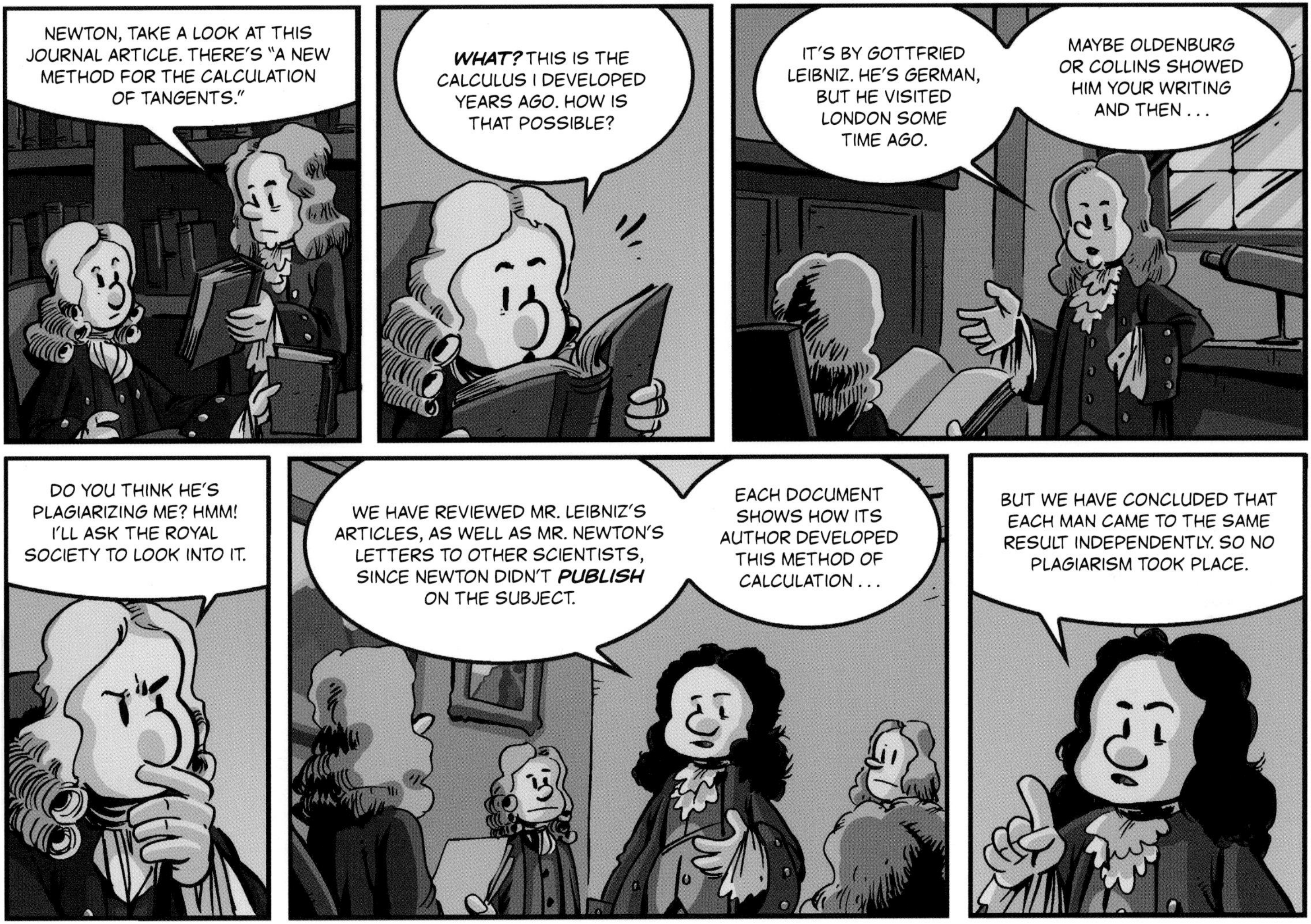
NEWTON, TAKE A LOOK AT THIS JOURNAL ARTICLE. THERE'S "A NEW METHOD FOR THE CALCULATION OF TANGENTS."
WHAT? THIS IS THE CALCULUS I DEVELOPED YEARS AGO. HOW IS THAT POSSIBLE?
IT'S BY GOTTFRIED LEIBNIZ. HE'S GERMAN, BUT HE VISITED LONDON SOME TIME AGO.
MAYBE OLDENBURG OR COLLINS SHOWED HIM YOUR WRITING AND THEN . . .
DO YOU THINK HE'S PLAGIARIZING ME? HMM! I'LL ASK THE ROYAL SOCIETY TO LOOK INTO IT.
WE HAVE REVIEWED MR. LEIBNIZ'S ARTICLES, AS WELL AS MR. NEWTON'S LETTERS TO OTHER SCIENTISTS, SINCE NEWTON DIDN'T *PUBLISH* ON THE SUBJECT.
EACH DOCUMENT SHOWS HOW ITS AUTHOR DEVELOPED THIS METHOD OF CALCULATION . . .
BUT WE HAVE CONCLUDED THAT EACH MAN CAME TO THE SAME RESULT INDEPENDENTLY. SO NO PLAGIARISM TOOK PLACE.

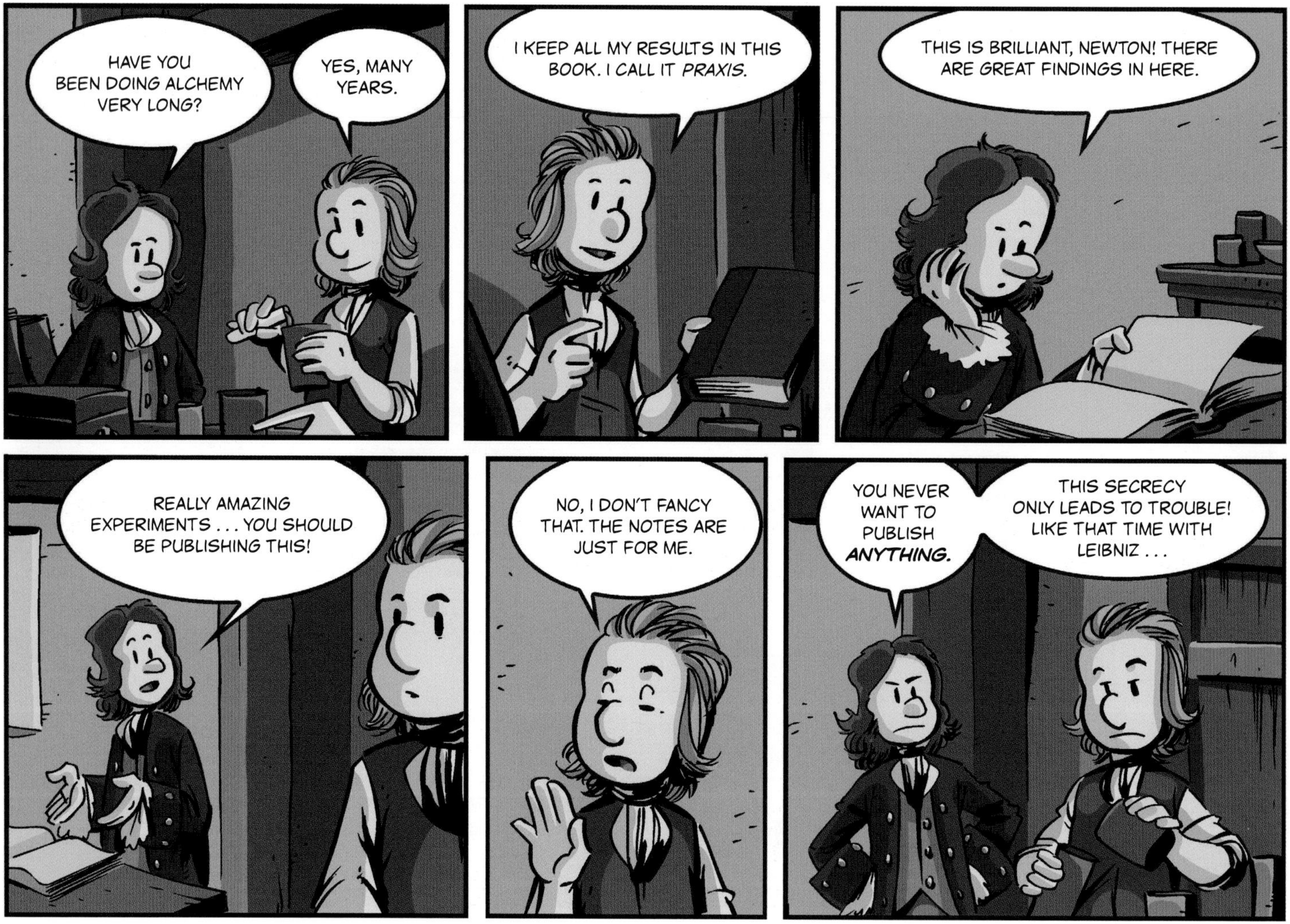
HAVE YOU BEEN DOING ALCHEMY VERY LONG?
YES, MANY YEARS.
I KEEP ALL MY RESULTS IN THIS BOOK. I CALL IT *PRAXIS.*
THIS IS BRILLIANT, NEWTON! THERE ARE GREAT FINDINGS IN HERE.
REALLY AMAZING EXPERIMENTS . . . YOU SHOULD BE PUBLISHING THIS!
NO, I DON'T FANCY THAT. THE NOTES ARE JUST FOR ME.
YOU NEVER WANT TO PUBLISH ***ANYTHING.***
THIS SECRECY ONLY LEADS TO TROUBLE! LIKE THAT TIME WITH LEIBNIZ . . .

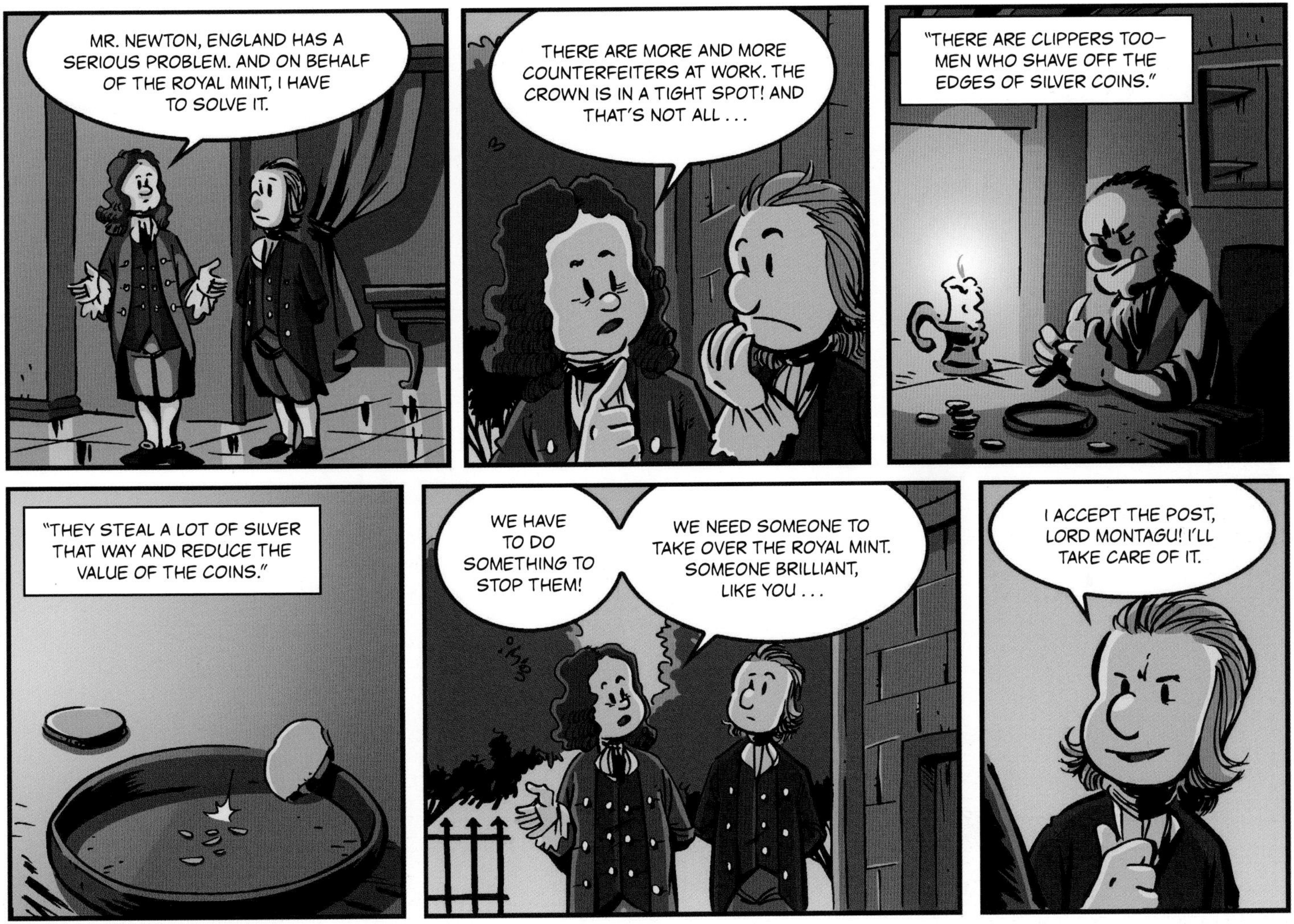
MR. NEWTON, ENGLAND HAS A SERIOUS PROBLEM. AND ON BEHALF OF THE ROYAL MINT, I HAVE TO SOLVE IT.
THERE ARE MORE AND MORE COUNTERFEITERS AT WORK. THE CROWN IS IN A TIGHT SPOT! AND THAT'S NOT ALL . . .
"THERE ARE CLIPPERS TOO—MEN WHO SHAVE OFF THE EDGES OF SILVER COINS."
"THEY STEAL A LOT OF SILVER THAT WAY AND REDUCE THE VALUE OF THE COINS."
WE HAVE TO DO SOMETHING TO STOP THEM!
WE NEED SOMEONE TO TAKE OVER THE ROYAL MINT. SOMEONE BRILLIANT, LIKE YOU . . .
I ACCEPT THE POST, LORD MONTAGU! I'LL TAKE CARE OF IT.

THE ROYAL MINT, TOWER OF LONDON, 1696

DO YOU SWEAR TO FULFILL YOUR DUTY AS WARDEN OF THE ROYAL MINT?

I DO!

AND NOW, FOLLOW ME. I'LL SHOW YOU OUR BEST-KEPT SECRET.

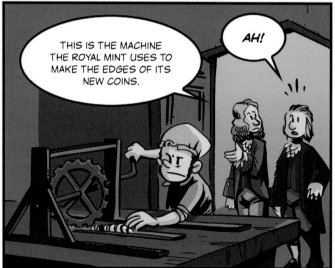

THIS IS THE MACHINE THE ROYAL MINT USES TO MAKE THE EDGES OF ITS NEW COINS.

AH!

THIS WAY, THEY ARE HARDER TO SHAVE, AND WE CAN FIND OUT MORE QUICKLY IF A COIN *HAS* BEEN SHAVED.

WHAT ARE YOU UP TO, MR. NEWTON?

I'M STUDYING EVERY DOCUMENT I CAN FIND ABOUT THE ROYAL MINT. I WANT TO KNOW EVERYTHING!

I HAVE HERE A STATEMENT THAT MUST BE SIGNED BY A REGRETFUL COUNTERFEITER. HE'S GOING TO INFORM ON HIS ACCOMPLICES.

I'LL TAKE CARE OF IT!

"I'LL HAVE HIM SIGN IT MYSELF . . ."

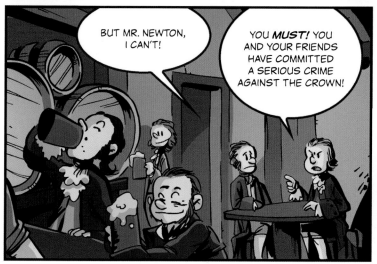

BUT MR. NEWTON, I CAN'T!

YOU **MUST!** YOU AND YOUR FRIENDS HAVE COMMITTED A SERIOUS CRIME AGAINST THE CROWN!

YOU'RE ALL GOING TO PRISON . . . BUT IF YOU SIGN THIS AND TESTIFY AGAINST THE OTHERS, MAYBE YOU'LL BE SPARED THE DUNGEONS.

GULP! ALL RIGHT . . . I'LL SIGN!

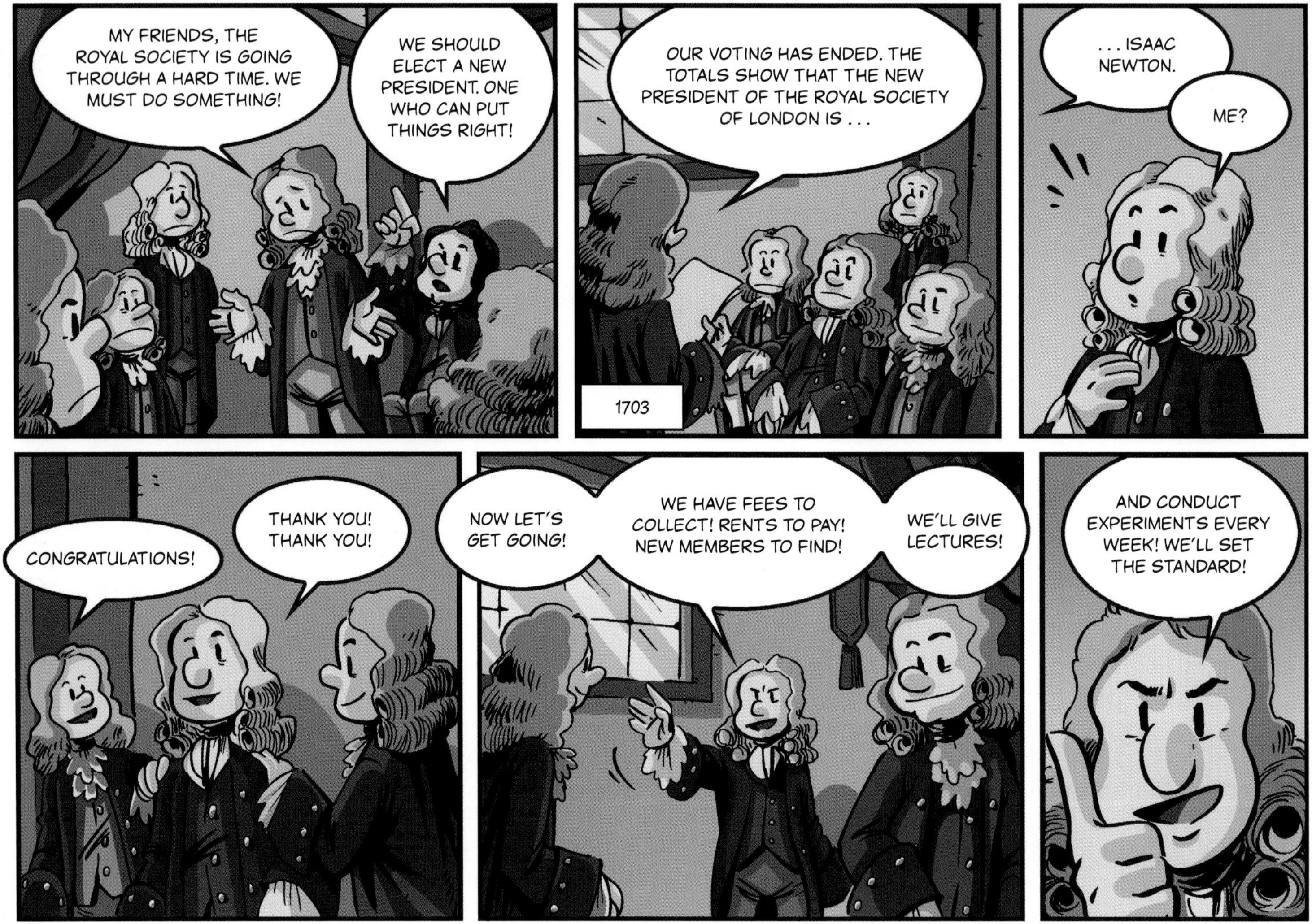
MY FRIENDS, THE ROYAL SOCIETY IS GOING THROUGH A HARD TIME. WE MUST DO SOMETHING!
WE SHOULD ELECT A NEW PRESIDENT. ONE WHO CAN PUT THINGS RIGHT!
OUR VOTING HAS ENDED. THE TOTALS SHOW THAT THE NEW PRESIDENT OF THE ROYAL SOCIETY OF LONDON IS . . .
1703
. . . ISAAC NEWTON.
ME?
CONGRATULATIONS!
THANK YOU! THANK YOU!
NOW LET'S GET GOING!
WE HAVE FEES TO COLLECT! RENTS TO PAY! NEW MEMBERS TO FIND!
WE'LL GIVE LECTURES!
AND CONDUCT EXPERIMENTS EVERY WEEK! WE'LL SET THE STANDARD!

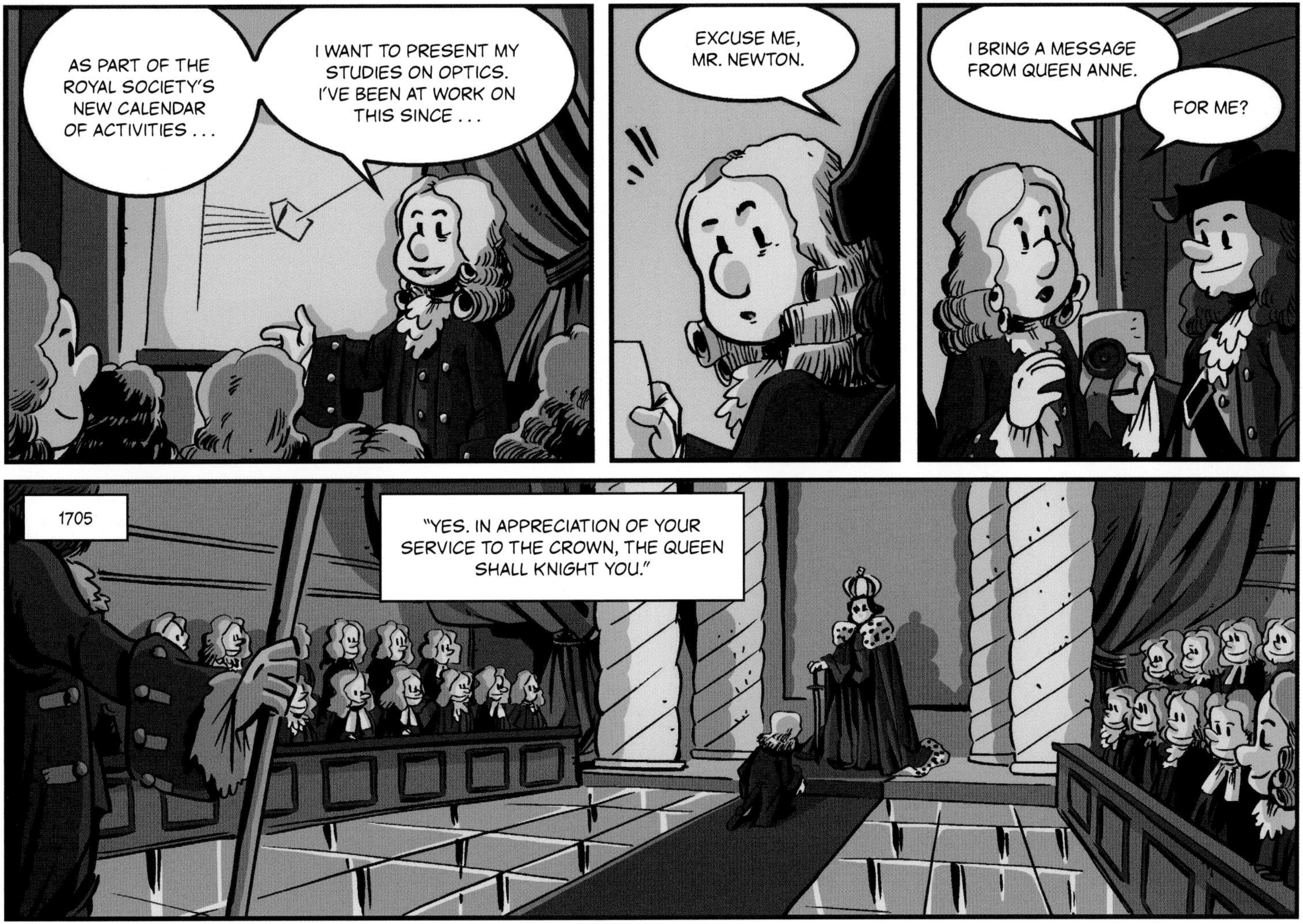
AS PART OF THE ROYAL SOCIETY'S NEW CALENDAR OF ACTIVITIES . . .
I WANT TO PRESENT MY STUDIES ON OPTICS. I'VE BEEN AT WORK ON THIS SINCE . . .
EXCUSE ME, MR. NEWTON.
I BRING A MESSAGE FROM QUEEN ANNE.
FOR ME?
1705
"YES. IN APPRECIATION OF YOUR SERVICE TO THE CROWN, THE QUEEN SHALL KNIGHT YOU."

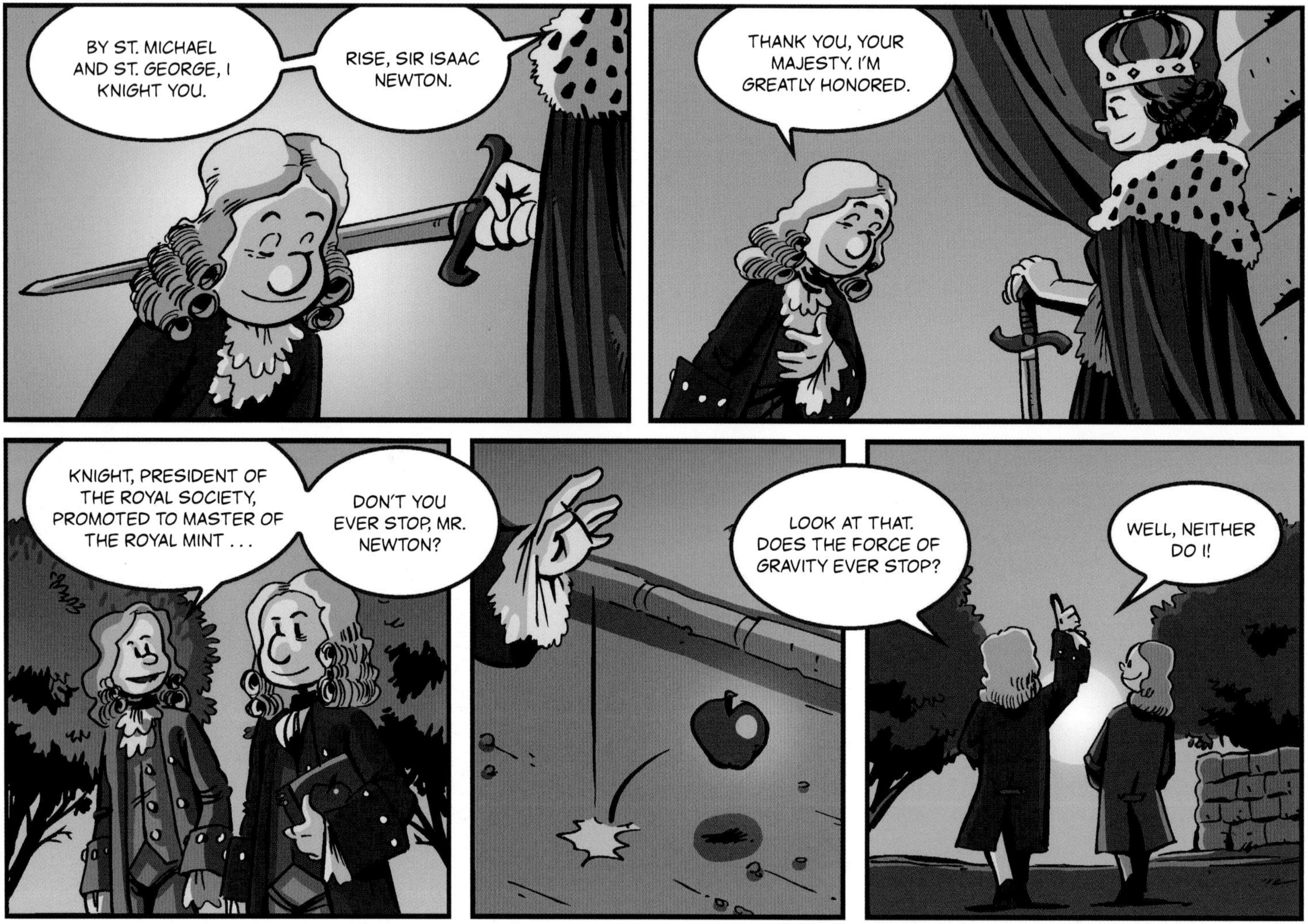
BY ST. MICHAEL AND ST. GEORGE, I KNIGHT YOU.
RISE, SIR ISAAC NEWTON.
THANK YOU, YOUR MAJESTY. I'M GREATLY HONORED.
KNIGHT, PRESIDENT OF THE ROYAL SOCIETY, PROMOTED TO MASTER OF THE ROYAL MINT . . .
DON'T YOU EVER STOP, MR. NEWTON?
LOOK AT THAT. DOES THE FORCE OF GRAVITY EVER STOP?
WELL, NEITHER DO I!

TIMELINE

1642   Isaac Newton is born in Woolsthorpe-by-Colsterworth, England, on December 25.

1655   He begins attending a boys' grammar school in nearby Grantham, England.

1661   He begins studying at Trinity College of the University of Cambridge in Cambridge, England.

1669   He is appointed a professor of mathematics at the University of Cambridge.

1671   He becomes a fellow of the Royal Society in London and shares his research with other scientists.

1675   He is granted permission to continue as a professor without becoming a priest.

1687   He publishes his most famous work, *Mathematical Principles of Natural Philosophy*.

1689   He becomes a member of Parliament in the British House of Commons.

1696   He is appointed Warden of the Royal Mint and fights the counterfeiting of English currency.

1703   He is elected president of the Royal Society of London.

1705   He is knighted by Queen Anne.

1727   He dies on March 20.

GLOSSARY

ALCHEMY: an early version of chemistry focused on transforming one substance into another

APOTHECARY: a person who sells medicine

COMPOSITION: the makeup of something

COUNTERFEITER: a criminal who creates fake money

FELLOW: a member of an organization. At a university, a fellow usually also belongs to the teaching staff.

FLUXIONS: Newton's term for calculus

HETEROGENEOUS: made up of dissimilar parts

HOMOGENOUS: made up of a single substance or common parts

OPTICS: the study of light and its properties

ORDAINED: to be made a priest or a minister

PLAGIARIST: a person who uses someone else's work without giving the person credit

PLAGUE: a contagious, widespread disease

PRISM: a transparent object, often with triangular bases, that reveals the spectrum of light

REFLECTING TELESCOPE: a telescope that uses a mirror or mirrors to collect and focus light

ROYAL MINT: the government office responsible for creating and managing England's money supply

ROYAL SOCIETY OF LONDON: a scientific institution founded in 1660; also known as the President, Council and Fellows of the Royal Society of London for Improving Natural Knowledge.

FURTHER RESOURCES

Bayarri, Jordi. *Albert Einstein and the Theory of Relativity*. Minneapolis: Graphic Universe, 2020.

"Isaac Newton: Illustrating History"
      https://www.youtube.com/watch?v=psMy-F8Llpg

"Isaac Newton: The Man Who Discovered Gravity"
      https://www.bbc.com/timelines/zwwgcdm

Latta, Sara, and Jeff Weigel. *Smash! Exploring the Mysteries of the Universe with the Large Hadron Collider*. Minneapolis: Graphic Universe, 2017.

Miller, Ron. *Recentering the Universe: The Radical Theories of Copernicus, Kepler, Galileo, and Newton*. Minneapolis: Twenty-First Century Books, 2014.

INDEX